Janice VanCleave's

Geometry for
Every Kid

Other Titles by Janice VanCleave

Science for Every Kid series:
Janice VanCleave's Astronomy for Every Kid
Janice VanCleave's Biology for Every Kid
Janice VanCleave's Chemistry for Every Kid
Janice VanCleave's Dinosaurs for Every Kid
Janice VanCleave's Earth Science for Every Kid
Janice VanCleave's Geography for Every Kid
Janice VanCleave's Math for Every Kid
Janice VanCleave's Physics for Every Kid

Spectacular Science Projects series:
Janice VanCleave's Animals
Janice VanCleave's Earthquakes
Janice VanCleave's Gravity
Janice VanCleave's Machines
Janice VanCleave's Magnets
Janice VanCleave's Microscopes and Magnifying Lenses
Janice VanCleave's Molecules
Janice VanCleave's Volcanoes

A+ series
Janice VanCleave's A+ Projects in Biology
Janice VanCleave's A+ Projects in Chemistry

Janice VanCleave's 200 Gooey, Slippery, Slimey, Wierd & Fun Experiments
Janice VanCleave's 201 Awesome, Magical, Bizarre & Incredible
Experiments

Janice VanCleave's

Geometry for Every Kid

Easy Activities that Make Learning Geometry Fun

John Wiley & Sons, Inc.
New York • Chichester • Brisbane • Tornoto • Singapore

Design and production by: WordCrafters Editorial Services, Inc.
Illustrator: Laurel Aiello

This text is printed on acid-free paper.

The publisher and the author have made every resonable effort to insure that the experiments and activities in this book are safe when conducted as instructed but assume no responsibility for any damage caused or sustained while performing the experiments or activities in this book. Parents, guardians, and/or teachers should supervise young readers who undertake the experiments and activities in this book.

Library of Congress Cataloging-in-Publication Data
VanCleave, Janice.
    Janice VanCleave's geometry for every kid   :   easy activities that
  make learning geometry fun   /   by Janice VanCleave.
        p.   cm.
    Includes index.
    ISBN 0-471-31142-1.—ISBN 0-471-31141-3 (pbk.)
    1. Geometry—Juvenile literature. [1. Geometry. 2. Mathematical
  recreations.]   I. Title.   II. Title: Geometry for every kid.
  QA445.5.V38   1994
  516—dc20   93-43049
                                                                              AC

Printed in the United States of America

10 9 8 7 6 5 4 3 2

This book is dedicated to two ladies who know all the angles of copyediting. They are a pleasure to work with, and I value our professional and personal relationship.

Nana Prior and Jude Patterson

I would be remiss in not extending the dedication to a special young lady who eagerly pretested many of the activities in this book. To my special laboratory assistant,

Kaitlin Patterson

Contents

Introduction

Geometry is the study of shapes. It uses numbers and symbols to describe the properties of these shapes and the relationships between them. This book explores two different kinds of geometry: **plane geometry**—the study of two-dimensional figures—and **solid geometry**—the study of three-dimensional figures. Why is understanding geometry important? Because questions such as What is its shape?, How big is it?, and Will it fit? are all part of everyday life. Geometry provides the skills needed to find the answers to such questions.

From the writings on sun-baked clay tablets found in Babylonian ruins, we learn that the people in this ancient culture surveyed their land. While doing this, they developed rules for measuring geometric shapes. These rules were not as exact as those that are used today. For example, Babylonians calculated the distance around a circle by multiplying its diameter by 3. Elementary schoolchildren today learn that this distance is more accurately determined by multiplying the circle's diameter by pi, which is approximately equal to 3.14.

Have we learned everything there is to know about geometry? No. Like all sciences, geometry is a constantly developing field of study. The more we learn about it, the more questions we think to ask. Comparing the shapes of puzzle pieces or deciding what size pizza to buy are only two of the ways you can develop the geometry skills that are so rewarding.

This book explains geometry's simple language in terms that you can easily learn and use. It teaches geometric concepts using examples that can be applied to many similar situations. The problems, experiments, and other application activities were selected because they can be explained using basic terms. One of the main objectives is to present the fun that can be had with geometry. So grab a pencil and lots of paper, and let the fun begin.

Read each of the 25 chapters slowly and follow all procedures carefully. You will learn best if each chapter is read in order, as there is some buildup of information as the book progresses. The format for each chapter is:

1. What You Need to Know: Background information and an explanation of terms.

2. Let's Think It Through: Questions to be answered or situations to be solved using the information from What You Need to Know.

3. Answers: Step-by-step instructions for solving the questions posed in Let's Think It Through.

4. Exercises: Practice problems to reinforce your skills.

5. Activity: A project to allow you to apply the skill to a problem-solving situation in the real world.

6. Solutions to Exercises: Step-by-step instructions for solving the Exercises.

7. Glossary: All **bold-faced** terms are defined in a Glossary at the end of the book. Be sure to flip back to the Glossary as often as necessary, making each term part of your personal vocabulary.

8. Some chapters also include a Mathematician's Toolbox with step-by-step instructions for making tools to use in the chapter.

General Instructions for Let's Think It Through and Exercise Sections

1. Study each question carefully by reading through it once or twice, then follow the steps described in the Answers.

2. Do the same thing for the Exercises, following the steps described in the Answers to the Let's Think It Through questions.

3. Check your answers in the Solutions to Exercises to evaluate your work.

4. Do the work again if any of your answers are incorrect.

General Instructions for Activity Sections

1. Read the Activity completely before starting.

2. Collect the supplies. You will have less frustration and more fun if all the necessary materials for the Activity are ready before you start. You lose your train of thought when you have to stop and search for supplies.

3. Do not rush through the Activity. Follow each step very carefully; never skip steps, and do not add your own. Safety is of utmost importance, and by reading each Activity before starting, and then following the instructions exactly, you can feel confident that no unexpected results will occur.

4. Observe. If your results are not the same as those described in the Activity, carefully reread the instructions, and start over from step 1.

1
Lineup

Identifying Lines,
Line Segments, and Rays

What You Need to Know

A line is a mark made by a pen, pencil, or other tool on a surface. This line can be of any shape and length. It can be straight or curved, such as a tracing around the fingers of your hand.

The geometric definition of a **line** is a straight path that has no definite length and goes on forever in both directions. In geometry, this continuation is indicated by an arrow at each end of the line. A geometrical line can be identified by naming any two points on the line, such as line TA (which can also be called line AT). The name of the line is read: line TA or line AT. It is written as: TA or AT.

A **line segment** is a part of a line. It follows a straight path between two points, called **endpoints**. A line segment is named by its endpoints. The name of the line segment in the example is read: line segment AB or line segment BA. It is written as: AB or BA.

A **ray** is a part of a line with one endpoint. It follows a straight path that goes on forever in only one direction. A ray's name starts with its endpoint. The name of the ray in the example is read: ray HL. It is written as: $\overrightarrow{HL}$.

Let's Think It Through

1. Identify the example that shows a line segment and give its name.

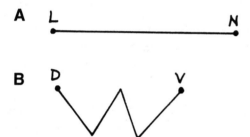

2. Identify the example that shows a ray and give its name.

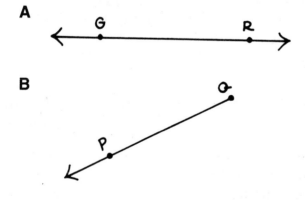

Answers

1. *Think!*

- Do both examples show straight paths? No, only example A shows a straight path.

- The endpoints on the line segment are L and N.

The name of the line segment is line segment LN ($\overline{LN}$) or line segment NL ($\overline{NL}$).

2. *Think!*

- A ray is a part of a line with one endpoint. Which example shows a line with a point at one end? Example B.

- The points on the ray, beginning with the endpoint, are Q and P.

The name of the ray is ray QP ($\overrightarrow{QP}$).

Exercises

1. Study the diagram and name the line segments.

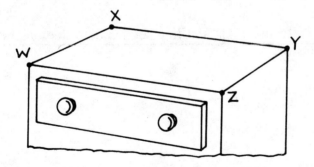

2. Does each example show a line? Answer yes or no for each example.

a. C   D

b.

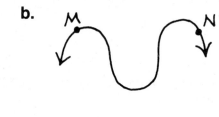

c.

3. Name the ray.

4. Name the line.

Activity: SIDE BY SIDE

Purpose To use lines and line segments to demonstrate an optical illusion.

Materials ruler
   pencil
   typing paper

Procedure

1. Use the ruler to draw a 6-inch (15-cm) line segment anywhere on the paper.

2. Mark a point in the exact center of the line. Label the endpoints K and M and the center point I as shown.

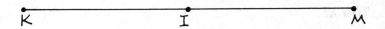

3. Draw two **V**'s pointing toward each other from points K and I. Draw a **V** pointing outward from point M as shown in the diagram.

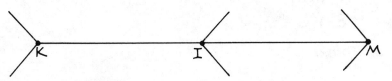

4. Compare the visual appearance of $\overline{KI}$ with that of $\overline{IM}$.

Results $\overline{KI}$ with the **V**'s pointing inward appears to be longer than $\overline{IM}$ even though we know that both lines are the same length.

Why?   Sometimes what we see is not what actually exists. A misleading image seen because of mistakes made by the brain is called an **optical illusion**. The direction of the **V**'s fools the brain into thinking that one line segment is longer than the other. $\overline{KI}$ appears longer because the **V**'s extend outward. The eyes follow these lines, and the interpretation in the brain is that this line segment is longer.

Solutions to Exercises

1. *Think!*

- Line segments have endpoints. The line segments that form the top of the chest are: $\overline{WX}$, $\overline{XY}$, $\overline{YZ}$, and $\overline{ZW}$ (or $\overline{XW}$, $\overline{YX}$, $\overline{ZY}$, and $\overline{WZ}$).

2. **Think!**

- For each example, ask yourself, Does this show a straight path with no endpoints?
    a. *No.*
    b. *No.*
    c. *Yes.*

3. **Think!**

- A ray's name starts with its endpoint.

The name of the ray is ray SC ($\overrightarrow{SC}$).

4. **Think!**

- A line is identified by naming two points on the line. The name can start with either of the two points.

The name of the line is line BC ($\overleftrightarrow{BC}$) or line CB ($\overleftrightarrow{CB}$).

2
What's the Angle?

Measuring Angles of Straight-Sided Figures

What You Need to Know

An **angle** is the figure formed when two rays that have the same endpoint or two straight lines meet. The rays or lines are the sides of the angle, and the endpoint where they meet is called the **vertex** of the angle. Three letters are used to name an angle, with the center letter being the vertex. The word *angle* can be replaced by its symbol: ∠. The name of the angle in the example is read: angle BEN or angle NEB. It is written as: ∠BEN or ∠NEB.

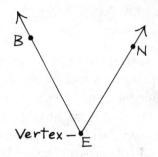

The unit used in measuring an angle is the degree. One degree is written as: 1°.

The measure of a **right angle** is 90 degrees. The corner of a rectangle is a right angle.

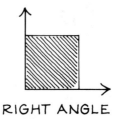

RIGHT ANGLE

The measure of an **acute angle** is less than 90 degrees.

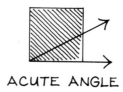

ACUTE ANGLE

The measure of an **obtuse angle** is greater than 90 degrees.

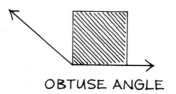

OBTUSE ANGLE

A **protractor** is an instrument used to measure angles in degrees. It is often shaped like a half circle. To measure an angle with a protractor, place the center mark of the protractor on the vertex of the angle and the straight edge on one side of the angle. The protractor will show two numbers on the curved edge where the second side crosses the scale. The sum of these two numbers will always equal 180 degrees. One of the numbers represents an acute angle, and the other an obtuse angle. If the angle is acute, use the smaller number. If it is obtuse, use the larger number. In the example, ray OT crosses the scale at

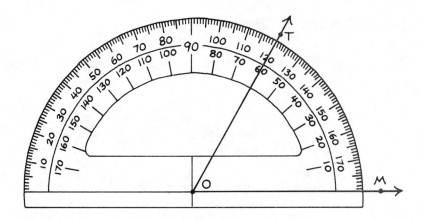

60 degrees and 120 degrees. Since the angle is acute, ∠TOM is 60 degrees.

A ruler or straightedge can be used when the sides of an angle are too short to cross the scale of the protractor. Lay the edge of the ruler along the side, and read the numbers where the ruler crosses the scale of the protractor. In the diagram, the edge of the ruler crosses the scale at 50 degrees and 130 degrees. The angle is obtuse, so ∠CAT is 130 degrees.

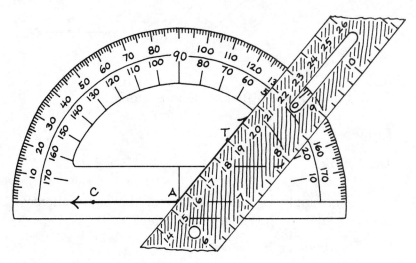

Let's Think It Through

1. Use a protractor to measure the angles in examples A and B.

A

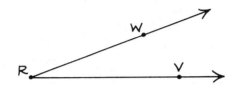

B

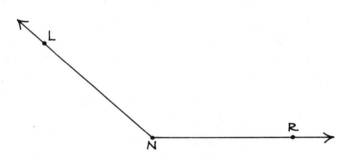

2. Write the name of the angle in example A.

Answers

1a. *Think!*

- The angle is acute. Which of the angle choices, 20 degrees or 160 degrees, is acute?

The angle is 20 degrees.

b.

- The angle is obtuse. Which of the angle choices, 40 degrees or 140 degrees, is obtuse?

The angle is 140 degrees.

2. *Think!*

- What are the angle's three letters, with the vertex letter in the middle? WRV.

- How is the angle read? Angle WRV or angle VRW.

The angle is written as: ∠WRV or ∠VRW.

Exercises

Use a protractor to measure each angle.

1. What is the angle of the bottom left corner of the picture frame?

2. Measure the angle of the lounge chair.

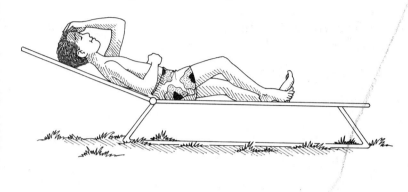

3. Measure and write the name of the angle.

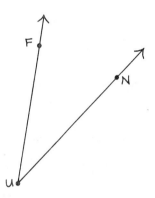

Activity: PAPER ART

Purpose To fold a sheet of paper into the shape of a whale.

Materials ruler
scissors
typing paper
blue crayon

Procedure

1. Measure and cut an 8-by-8-inch (20-by-20-cm) square from the paper.

2. Color one side of the paper blue.

3. Lay the paper on a table, white side up.

4. Fold the paper in half diagonally from point A to point B to form a center fold line.

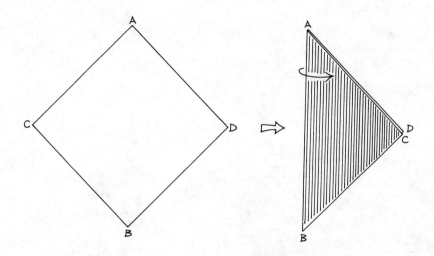

5. Unfold the paper and cut about 2 inches (5 cm) down the center fold line from point A toward point B.

6. Fold the paper so that points C and D meet at the center fold line.

7. Fold the paper again, so that points E and F meet at the center fold line.

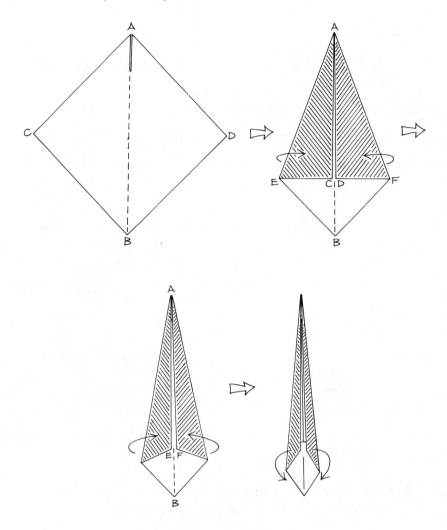

8. Refold along the fold line from point A to point B.

9. Fold the two cut ends outward.

10. Turn the paper over and draw an eye and a mouth on either side of the face, as in the diagram.

Results   You have made a paper whale.

Why?   Each fold in the paper is made at a new angle. The art of folding paper into shapes that look like objects is called **origami** and was originated by the Chinese about 2,000 years ago. In the seventh century this art form was brought to Japan, where Japanese magicians introduced the seeming magic of making a few simple folds to produce birds, animals, boats, and other pretty forms to delight their audiences. Origami is now a universal word for the art of paper folding.

Solutions to Exercises

1. *Think!*

   • The frame is a rectangle. Rectangles have what type of angles? Right angles.

   • How many degrees are in a right angle?

   The bottom left corner of the frame is 90 degrees.

2. *Think!*

   • The angle is obtuse. Which of the angle choices, 20 degrees or 160 degrees, is obtuse?

   The angle of the lounge chair is 160 degrees.

3. *Think!*

   • The angle is acute. Which of the angle choices, 35 degrees or 145 degrees, is acute?

   Angle FUN (∠FUN) or angle NUF (∠NUF) is 35 degrees.

3
Crossover

Identifying Intersecting, Parallel, and Perpendicular Lines

What You Need to Know

Lines that meet or cross each other and have only one point in common are called **intersecting lines**. In the example, lines CD and EG intersect, with F as the common point.

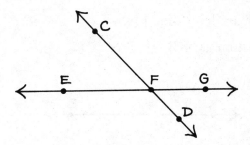

Two lines that intersect to form a right angle are **perpendicular lines**. To indicate that lines are perpendicular to each other, a square can be drawn around the point where the lines intersect, or a single square can be drawn in one corner. In the example on the next page, lines GH and IJ intersect, and as indicated by the square, the lines are perpendicular to each other. They are read: Line GH is perpendicular to line IJ.

They are written as: $\overleftrightarrow{GH} \perp \overleftrightarrow{IJ}$.

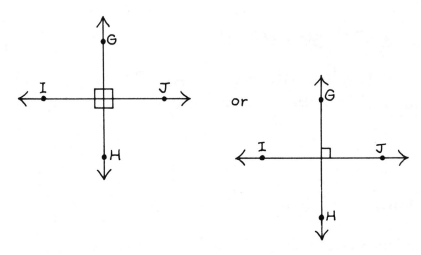

Lines that do not intersect and are always the same distance apart are called **parallel lines**. Lines KB and FN are examples of parallel lines. They are read:

Line KB is parallel to line FN.

They are written as: $\overleftrightarrow{KB} \parallel \overleftrightarrow{FN}$.

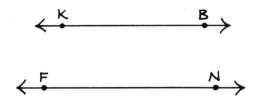

Let's Think It Through

Identify the intersecting and parallel lines or line segments in the three examples.

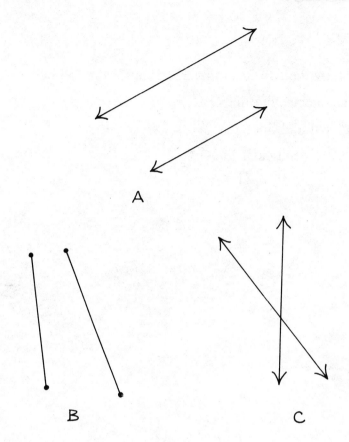

Answer

Think!

- The lines in example A do not meet or cross and are the same distance apart.

A is an example of parallel lines.

- The line segments in example B do not meet or cross and are not the same distance apart. They are neither parallel nor intersecting lines.

- The lines in example C cross.

C is an example of intersecting lines.

Exercise

1. Study the two diagrams and identify the following:

   a. intersecting lines

   b. parallel lines

   c. perpendicular lines

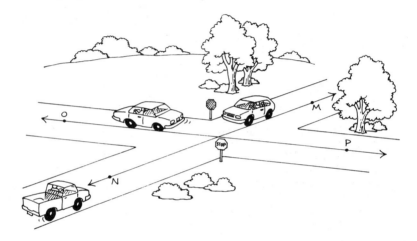

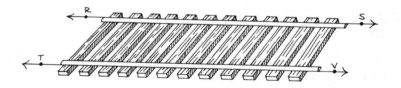

Activity: BALANCING NAILS

Purpose To show how six intersecting and parallel nails can balance on the head of a seventh vertical nail.

Materials hammer
seven 16d nails
2-by-4-by-6-inch (5-by-10-by-15-cm) or larger
wooden block
adult helper

Procedure

1. Ask your helper to hammer the tip of one of the nails into the center of the wooden block. The nail should be as firm and vertical as possible without being driven in too deeply.

2. Arrange the nails so that they work as a single unit by following these steps. The numbers refer to the nails as shown in the diagrams:

- Lay nail 1 parallel with the edge of the table.

- Lay nails 2, 3, 4, and 5 over nail 1 so that they are parallel with each other and their heads slightly extend past the sides of nail 1.

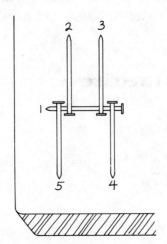

- Lay nail 6 on top of the arrangement so that it is parallel with nail 1 and its tip points in the opposite direction of the tip of nail 1.

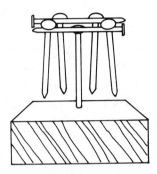

3. Gently and very carefully pick up the group of nails by holding the ends of nails 1 and 6 with your thumbs and index fingers.

4. Place the center of nail 1 on the head of the vertical nail that is in the wooden block. This may take some practice.

Results   The arrangement of nails balances.

Why?   The weight of each nail is the same. Thus, the weights of the two sets of hanging parallel nails counterbalance each other, as do the weights of the two horizontal parallel nails. This counterbalancing of weight allows six nails to balance on the head of one nail.

Solution to Exercise

1a. *Think!*

- Which lines cross?

$\overleftrightarrow{MN}$ intersects $\overleftrightarrow{OP}$.

b. *Think!*

- Which lines do not cross, run in the same direction, and are always the same distance apart?

$\overleftrightarrow{RS}$ || $\overleftrightarrow{TV}$.

c. *Think!*

- Do any of the lines meet or intersect at 90 degrees? No.

There are no perpendicular lines in either diagram.

4
Three-Sided Figures
Identifying Triangles

What You Need to Know

A **plane figure** is a geometric figure that lies on a flat surface.
A **closed figure** is a geometric figure that begins and ends at
the same point. A **polygon** is a closed plane figure formed by
three or more line segments that are joined only at the endpoints, or vertices, with each endpoint connected to only two
line segments. In the diagram, figure A is the only example of
a polygon.

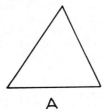

A

B

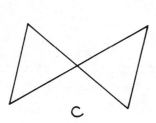

C

The different types of polygons are identified by the number of their sides. A polygon made up of three sides is called a **triangle**. The sum of the angles created by the three sides is always 180 degrees.

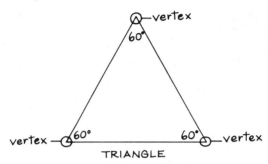

Triangles can be identified in two different ways. One way depends on whether the length of their sides is **congruent** (the same). In an **equilateral triangle**, all three sides are congruent. In an **isosceles triangle**, two sides are congruent. In the **scalene triangle**, no sides are congruent.

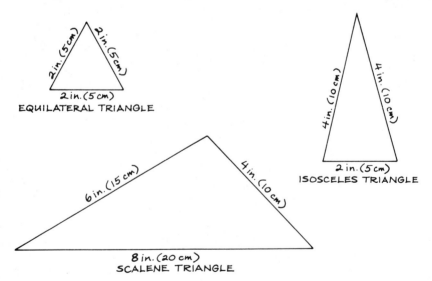

The second way of identifying triangles depends on the size of their angles. In an **acute triangle**, all angles measure less than 90 degrees. In a **right triangle**, one angle measures exactly 90 degrees. (Note in the figure that a small square is placed in the corner to identify the right angle.) In an **obtuse triangle**, one angle measures greater than 90 degrees.

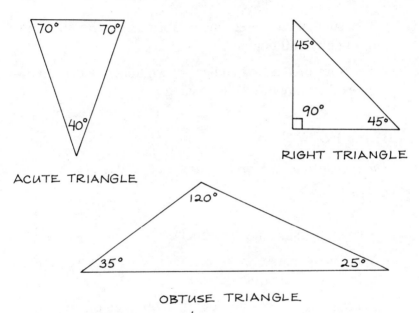

ACUTE TRIANGLE

RIGHT TRIANGLE

OBTUSE TRIANGLE

Let's Think It Through

Look at the pennant in the diagram and answer the following:

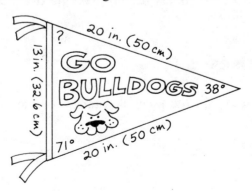

1. What is the measure of the missing angle?

2. What are all the possible names for the triangle?

Answers

1. *Think!*

- The sum of the three angles formed by the sides of a triangle is 180 degrees.

- The sum of the two angles shown subtracted from 180 gives the amount of the missing angle:

$71° + 38° = 109°$
$180° - 109° = ?$

The measure of the missing angle is 71 degrees.

2. *Think!*

- Two of the sides are congruent.

- What is the name given to a triangle with two congruent sides? Isosceles triangle.

- All the angles measure less than 90 degrees.

- What is the name given to a triangle in which all angles measure less than 90 degrees? Acute triangle.

The possible names for the triangle are isosceles triangle and acute triangle.

Exercises

1. What are all the possible names for the boat's triangular sail?

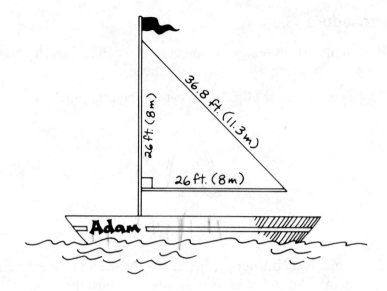

2. Use the angles given and the scale for each side to determine all the possible names for the triangle shown here.

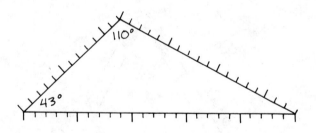

Activity: STRAW TRIANGLES

Purpose To construct models of acute triangles.

Materials scissors
4 plastic drinking straws
ruler
6 small paper clips

Procedure

1. Cut the straws into six pieces: make one 2-inch (5-cm) piece and five 4-inch (10-cm) pieces.

2. Open the paper clips as shown in the diagram.

3. To make each triangle, insert one bent end of each paper clip into the end of each straw piece. Adjust the angle of the bent paper clip if needed. Make two triangles by using the following straw length combinations:

- Three 4-inch (10-cm)

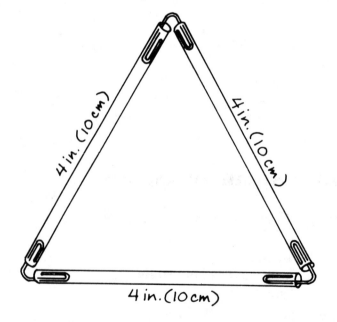

4 in. (10 cm)

• Two 4-inch (10-cm) and one 2-inch (5-cm)

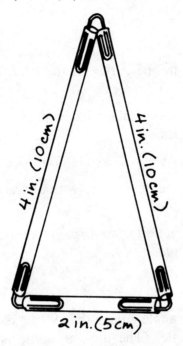

Results   Two acute triangles are formed. One of the triangles is equilateral and the other, isosceles.

Why?   The lengths of the straws determine the angles formed when the straws are connected. The triangle formed by connecting three straws of equal length produces an equilateral acute triangle. The angles of this triangle are congruent and each is 60 degrees. Replacing one of the straws with a shorter straw produces an isosceles triangle. The shorter straw pulls the two longer straws closer together and decreases the angle between them. The other two angles in the triangle increase, but neither is 90 degrees or greater. Thus, both triangles are acute.

Solutions to Exercises

1. *Think!*

- The square in one corner of the triangle indicates that the angle is 90 degrees.

- What are triangles called that have one 90-degree angle? Right triangles.

- The lengths of two sides are congruent.

- What is a triangle having two congruent sides called? Isosceles triangle.

The possible names for the triangle are right triangle and isosceles triangle.

2. *Think!*

- There is one angle greater than 90 degrees. Thus, it is an obtuse triangle. (The missing angle is not needed to identify the triangle.)

- How many sections are on the scale for each side of the triangle? 12, 18, and 25.

- None of the sides are congruent. Thus, the triangle is scalene.

The possible names for the triangle are obtuse triangle and scalene triangle.

5

Four-Sided Figures

Identifying Quadrilaterals

What You Need to Know

A **quadrilateral** is a four-sided polygon formed by four line segments. There are three basic types of quadrilaterals: the **trapezium**, which has no parallel sides; the **trapezoid**, which has one pair of parallel sides; and the **parallelogram**, which has two pairs of parallel sides.

An **isosceles trapezoid** is a special type of trapezoid whose two nonparallel sides are congruent. Rhomboid, rhombus, rectangle, and square are all examples of parallelograms. A **rhomboid** is a parallelogram that has no right angles and only opposite sides are congruent; a **rhombus** is a parallelogram that has no right angles and four congruent sides; and a **rectangle** is a parallelogram that has four right angles and only opposite sides are congruent. A **square** is a special type of rectangle that has four congruent sides. Even though each of these figures is an example of a parallelogram, the name *parallelogram* is commonly used to identify only the rhomboid.

While a rhomboid is commonly called a parallelogram, it will be called a rhomboid in this book to distinguish it from the other members of the parallelogram family.

QUADRILATERALS

Types	Examples
Trapezium	
Trapezoid family	trapezoid Isosceles trapezoid
Parallelogram family	rhomboid rhombus rectangle square

Let's Think It Through

Study the diagram and answer these questions:

1. How many quadrilaterals are labeled in the diagram?

2. How many of the quadrilaterals are parallelograms?

3. Identify each of the quadrilaterals.

Answers

1. *Think!*

- Which figures have four sides?

There are three quadrilaterals: figures A, B, and C.

2. *Think!*

- How many of these figures have two pairs of parallel sides?

Two of the figures are parallelograms: A and C.

3. *Think!*

- Figure A is a parallelogram with four right angles and four congruent sides.

Figure A is a square.

- Figure B has only one pair of parallel sides and the two nonparallel sides are congruent.

Figure B is an isosceles trapezoid.

- Figure C is a parallelogram that has four right angles and only opposite sides are congruent.

Figure C is a rectangle.

Exercise

Identify the four labeled quadrilaterals in the diagram.

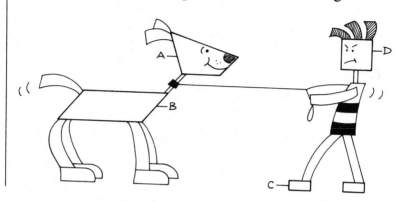

Activity: REARRANGEMENT

Purpose To compare the shapes of a rhomboid and a rectangle.

Materials 1 yellow and 1 blue transparent plastic report folder
marking pen
ruler
scissors

Procedure

1. Lay the yellow plastic folder over the rectangle pattern shown.

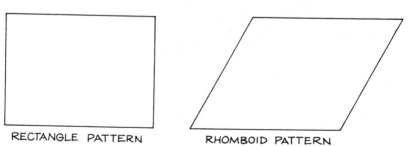

RECTANGLE PATTERN   RHOMBOID PATTERN

2. Trace the rectangle figure onto the plastic. Use the edge of the ruler to make the edges of the rectangle straight.

3. Cut out the traced rectangle.

4. Lay the blue plastic folder over the rhomboid pattern and trace the figure onto the plastic.

5. Cut out the traced rhomboid.

6. Lay the rhomboid on top of the rectangle as shown.

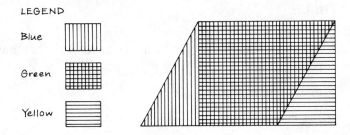

LEGEND

Blue

Green

Yellow

7. Place the edge of the ruler on the right side of the blue triangle and trace this side.

8. Cut off the blue triangle and place it over the yellow triangle as shown.

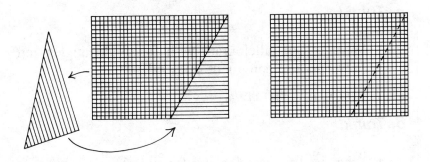

Results   The rhomboid is taken apart and rearranged to form a rectangle of equal size.

Why? The rhomboid is like a flexible rectangle with its top pushed to one side and its bottom pushed to the other. The shape of the rhomboid can be changed into that of an equal-size rectangle by cutting off the blue triangle sticking out on one side and placing it over the yellow triangle on the opposite side. This makes a green rectangle.

Solutions to Exercise

1a. *Think!*

- What is the name given a quadrilateral that has no parallel sides?

Figure A is a trapezium.

b. *Think!*

- A quadrilateral with four parallel sides is called a parallelogram.
- What is a parallelogram with no right angles called?

Figure B is a rhomboid, more commonly called a parallelogram.

c. *Think!*

- What is a parallelogram with four right angles and only opposite congruent sides called?

Figure C is a rectangle.

d. *Think!*

- What is the special name for a rectangle with four congruent sides?

Figure D is a square.

6
Hidden Figures

Determining Different Ways that Polygons Can Fit Together

What You Need to Know

As you learned in the previous chapters, polygons are closed plane figures with straight sides. The simplest polygon, called a triangle, has three sides. Rhomboids, squares, and rectangles are examples of polygons with four sides.

With their straight sides made by line segments, small polygons can fit together to form larger figures of various shapes. Triangles can fit together to form not only larger triangles, but also diamonds, squares, trapezoids, and other multisided figures, such as **pentagons**, which have five sides, and **hexagons**, which have six sides. There are many other possibilities.

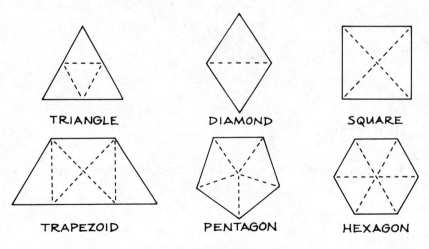

TRIANGLE   DIAMOND   SQUARE

TRAPEZOID   PENTAGON   HEXAGON

Let's Think It Through

How many squares are hidden in the figure?

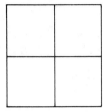

Answer

Think!

- A square has four congruent sides and all its angles are right angles.
- The figure shows one large square made up of four smaller squares.

The total number of squares is five.

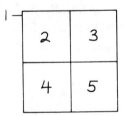

Exercises

1. Study the triangle in the figure to answer questions a and b.

a. How many triangles can you find in the figure?

b. How many hidden diamonds can you find in the figure?

2. Study the figure of the square to determine the total number of squares.

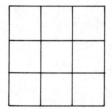

Activity: CUTAWAY

Purpose To make a tangram.

Materials ruler
scissors
sheet of construction paper
stopwatch

Procedure

1. Measure and cut an 8-by-8-inch (20-by-20-cm) square from the paper.

2. Follow these steps to divide the square into seven pieces. Number each piece as shown in the diagrams.

   • Cut the square in half diagonally to form two separate triangles, and label the pieces "1" and "2."

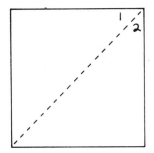

- Cut piece 1 in half as shown and label the second triangular piece "3." Place both small triangles aside.

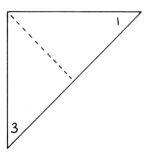

- Fold the corner of piece 2 so that the corner opposite the longest side touches the center of the longest side. Unfold and cut along the fold line. Piece 2 is now a trapezoid. Label the triangular piece "4" and set it aside.

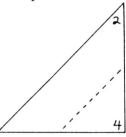

- Fold the trapezoid (piece 2) in half so that the shorter sides match up. Unfold and cut along the fold line. Label the cutoff half piece "5," and set it aside.

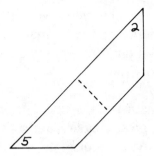

- Fold piece 2 so that the pointed end touches the opposite corner. Unfold and cut along the fold line. Label the square piece "6." Set pieces 2 and 6 aside.

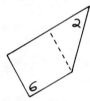

- Fold piece 5 so that side A in the figure touches side B. Unfold and cut along the fold line. Label the triangular piece "7." Set pieces 7 and 5 aside.

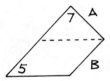

3. Without looking at the diagrams in this book, time how long it takes you to arrange the seven pieces to make the original square.

4. Try making different shaped polygons with the pieces.

Results   The square is cut into seven pieces: five triangles—two large, one medium, and two small; one square; and one rhomboid. The time it takes to arrange the pieces into a square varies with each individual.

Why?   A **tangram** is a Chinese puzzle made by cutting a square into five triangles, a square, and a rhomboid. The pieces can be arranged to form the original square as well as a great variety of other polygons.

Solutions to Exercises

1a. *Think!*

- What is the shape of a triangle? A closed figure with three straight sides.
- The figure shows a large triangle with four smaller hidden triangles inside.

The total number of triangles in the figure is five.

b. *Think!*

- A diamond shape can be formed by combining two equal-size triangles.
- How many pairs of triangles make up the figure?

The total number of hidden diamonds in the figure is three.

2. *Think!*

- The figure shows one square with nine smaller squares inside.

- Each group of four small squares makes one larger square. How many different groups of four squares are hidden in the diagram? Four.

- $1 + 9 + 4 = 14$

The total number of squares in the figure is fourteen.

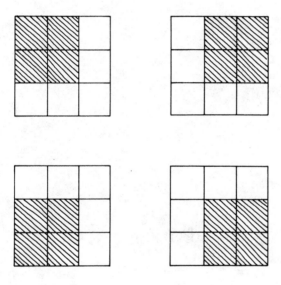

7
Overlay

Identifying Congruent Polygons

What You Need to Know

Congruent polygons are polygons that are exactly the same shape and size. The congruency of two polygons is determined by laying one polygon on top of another to determine if each side and vertex (the point where two sides of the polygon meet) matches with a corresponding side and vertex on the other polygon.

Figures A and B are congruent polygons because they are exactly the same shape and size. If A were placed on top of B, the sides and vertices of both figures would exactly line up.

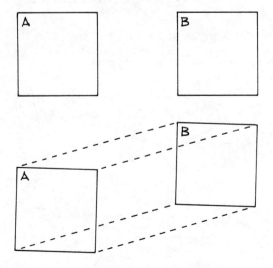

Figures C and D are not congruent polygons. They have the same shape, but C is smaller than D. If C were placed on top of D, their sides and vertices would not match.

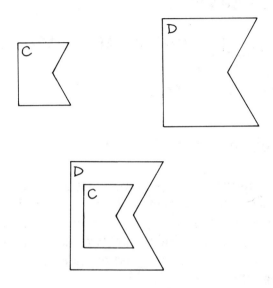

Let's Think It Through

Study figures E, F, and G to answer the following:

1. Is polygon E congruent to polygon F?

2. Is polygon E congruent to polygon G?

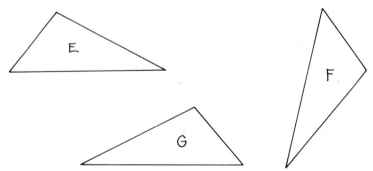

Answer

1. *Think!*

- To compare the figures, use tracing paper to neatly trace polygon E. Slide and rotate the tracing to fit over polygon F.

- Do the figures exactly fit on top of each other with their vertices and sides matching? Yes.

Polygons E and F are congruent.

2. *Think!*

- Flip the tracing of polygon E over, then slide and rotate it so that it fits over polygon G.

- Do the sides and vertices of the two polygons match? Yes.

Polygons E and G are congruent.

Exercise

Use a tracing of polygon A to help you find congruent polygons in the diagram on the next page.

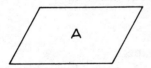

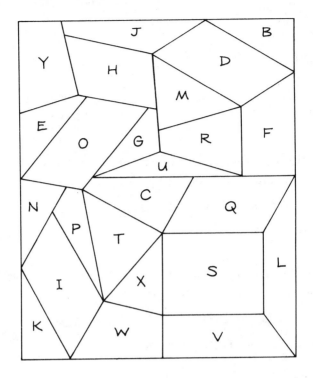

Activity: MATCHUP

Purpose To construct a design with congruent polygons.

Materials pencil
tracing paper
yellow, red, green, and white construction paper
scissors
glue

Procedure

1. Follow the steps below to cut two polygons congruent to figure A from the yellow paper.

• Trace figure A on the tracing paper.

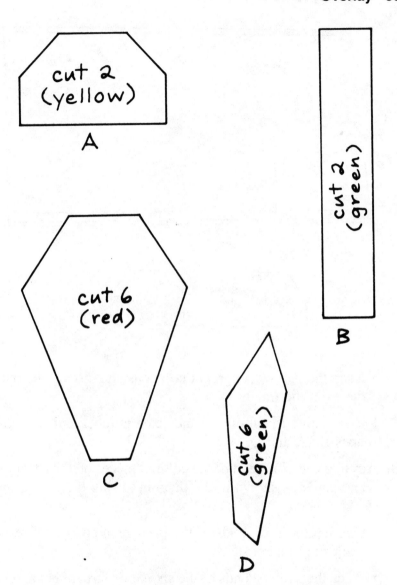

cut 2
(yellow)

A

cut 2
(green)

B

cut 6
(red)

C

cut 6
(green)

D

- Fold the yellow construction paper in half.
- Place the traced pattern of figure A on the folded paper.
- Cut out the design by cutting through the tracing paper and the folded yellow paper.

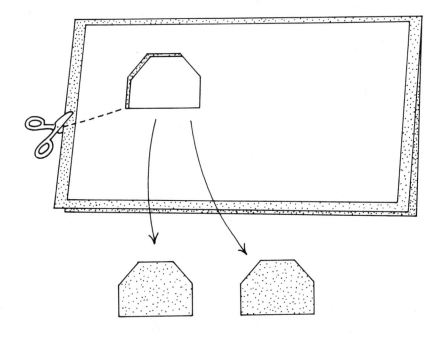

- Keep the yellow congruent polygons and discard the one cut from the tracing paper.

2. Repeat step 1 to cut out the indicated number and color of shapes B, C, and D.

3. Arrange and glue each of the colored pieces on the sheet of white paper as shown in the diagram, using the following steps:

- Overlap the short ends of the two green congruent rectangles to make a stem.

- Place the shortest ends of the six red congruent hexagons together in the shape of flower petals.

- Flip one of the yellow hexagons upside down and place the two in the center of the petals so that the long sides of the hexagons touch.

- Place one of the six green pentagons on the right side of the stem to make a leaf that angles upward toward the petals. Flip a second pentagon leaf over and place it on the left side of the stem opposite the first leaf. Arrange the remaining four green pentagons at the base of the stem to make blades of grass.

Results   A colored flower design is created.

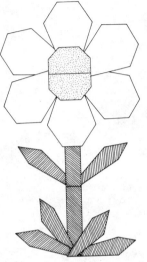

Why?   Cutting out the polygons by cutting through the tracing paper and the folded construction paper produces three congruent polygons, one from the tracing paper and two from the construction paper. Although rotating or flipping the designs can change their alignment, it does not change their shape or size. Thus, they remain congruent polygons.

Solution to Exercise

Think!

- To compare the figures, use tracing paper to neatly trace polygon A. Slide, rotate, or flip the tracing to compare it with the polygons in the diagram.

- Which polygons does polygon A exactly fit on top of so that their vertices and sides match?

Polygons D, I, O, and Q are congruent with polygon A.

8
Five-Square Figures
Making Pentominoes

What You Need to Know

A figure made from five congruent squares is called a **pentomino**. The squares must be arranged so that the entire side of one square lines up with the whole side of the square it touches. The diagram shows figures made with five squares and identifies the correct arrangement of pentominoes and incorrect arrangements that are not pentominoes.

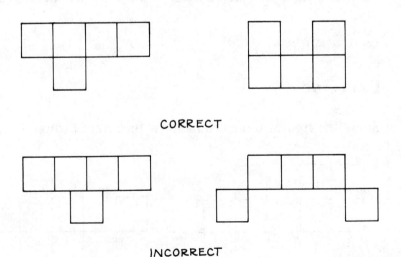

CORRECT

INCORRECT

Let's Think It Through

Which one of the figures is an example of a pentomino?

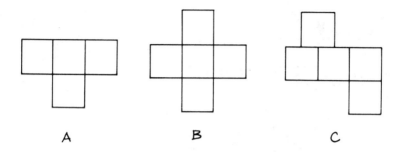

A   B   C

Answer

Think!

- Pentominoes are made up of five squares. Do any of the figures have five squares? Yes, B and C.

- In which figure do the entire sides of touching squares line up?

Figure B is a pentomino.

Exercise

Study the figures to determine how many are pentominoes.

A   B   C

Activity: SQUARE DANCE

Purpose   To determine the 12 different possible pentominoes.

Materials   ruler
scissors
1 sheet of construction paper
6 sheets of typing paper

Procedure

1. Measure and cut five 1-by-1-inch (2.5-by-2.5-cm) squares from the construction paper.

2. Place the five colored squares on one sheet of typing paper.

3. Arrange the squares into a pentomino.

4. Trace around the outside of each square.

5. Rearrange the five squares on the same paper to form a second pentomino.

6. Again, trace around the outside of each square.

7. Repeat the procedure of arranging the squares into other pentominoes and tracing around them until 12 different pentominoes are drawn, two on each sheet of paper.

Results Diagrams of the 12 possible pentominoes are created.

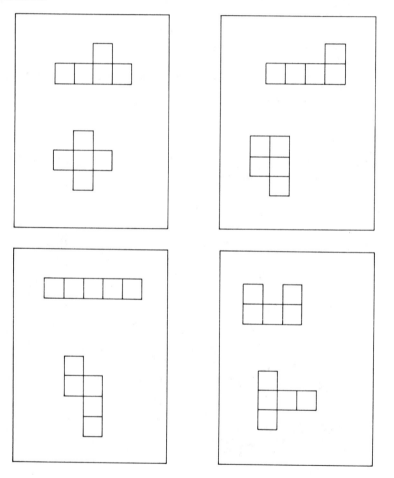

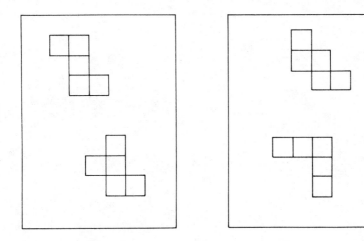

Why?   Only 12 different pentominoes can be created. Rearrangements of the pentominoes, such as flipping them upside down or rotating them, are not counted as new shapes.

Solution to Exercise

Think!

- How many figures are made with five squares? Three.
- In which figure do the entire sides of touching squares line up? B.

Only one of the figures is a pentomino.

9
Curvey Figures
Learning about Curved Geometric Figures

What You Need to Know

Geometric figures that do not have straight sides are called **curved figures**. Curved figures can be closed or open. **Closed curves** are continuous; they do not have a break in the line forming their **perimeter** (the outer boundary of a plane figure). The ends of the lines forming **open curves** do not meet, because the lines are not continuous.

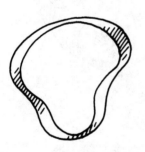

CLOSED CURVE

OPEN CURVE

If the perimeter of a curved figure does not intersect (cross) itself, the curve is said to be a **simple curve**. The perimeter of a **complex curve** does intersect itself. The diagram shows examples of different curved figures, including a **circle**, which is a simple closed curve. Unlike other simple closed curves, the distance between the center of a circle and any point on its perimeter, called the **circumference**, is always the same.

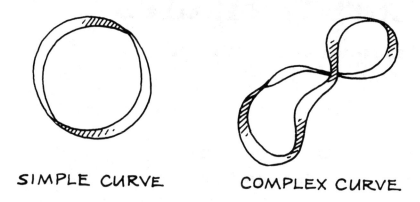

SIMPLE CURVE   COMPLEX CURVE

Let's Think It Through

Match the picture with the correct description.

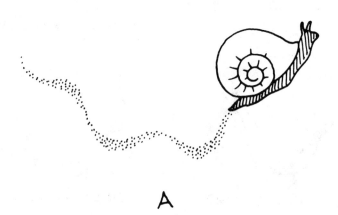

A

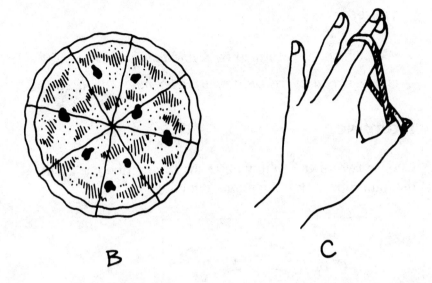

B   C

1. a simple closed curve

2. an open curve

3. a curve whose perimeter intersects itself

Answers

1. *Think!*

- Which curved figure has a perimeter that does not intersect itself and is continuous?

Figure B is a simple closed curve.

2. *Think!*

- Which curved figure is formed by a line that has ends that
do not meet?

Figure A is an open curve.

3. *Think!*

- Which curve is formed by a line that crosses itself?

Figure C is a curve whose perimeter intersects itself.

Exercise

Choose two of the following terms to describe each curved diagram: open, closed, simple, complex.

1.

2.

3.

Activity: TWISTERS

Purpose To predict and compare the results of cutting two different closed-curved paper strips down their centers.

Materials ruler
scissors
butcher paper
pencil
transparent tape

Procedure

1. Measure and cut two separate 2-by-36-inch (5-cm-by-1-m) strips from the butcher paper.

2. Label the strips 1 and 2.

3. Prepare strip 1 by taping the ends together to make a simple closed curve.

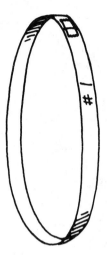

4. Prepare strip 2 by holding the ends, adding a twist to the paper by turning one end 180 degrees, and then taping the ends together to make a complex closed curve.

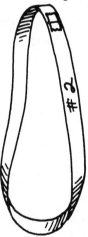

5. Lay strip 1 over the corner of a table. Starting where the edges are taped together, draw a zigzag line back and forth down the strip until you return to the starting point.

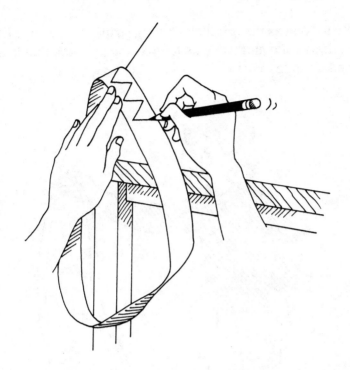

6. Repeat step 4, using strip 2.

7. Without removing the tape, cut along the center of each strip parallel with the edges.

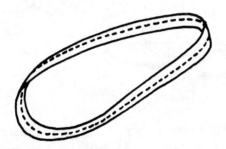

Results The zigzag marking appears only on one side of strip 1, but on both sides of strip 2. Cutting strip 1 along the center splits the strips into two identical rings, half as wide and equally as long as the original. Cutting strip 2 creates one large ring, half as wide and twice as long as the original, that is also a closed complex curve.

Why?   Twisting the paper 180 degrees creates a complex closed curve known as the **Möbius strip**, named after its discoverer, August Ferdinand Möbius (1790-1868). The reason the Möbius strip does not separate into two rings when it is cut in half is that the twisting produces a ring with only one side—the inside is also the outside.

Solutions to Exercises

1. *Think!*

- Is there a break in the perimeter of the lake? No.
- Does the line forming the figure intersect itself? No.

The figure is a simple closed curve.

2. *Think!*

- Is there a break in the perimeter of the jump rope? Yes.
- Does the line forming the figure intersect itself? No.

The figure is a simple open curve.

3. *Think!*

- Is there a break in the perimeter of the ice pattern? No.
- Does the line forming the figure intersect itself? Yes.

The figure is a closed complex curve.

10
Never-Ending Line

Identifying and Drawing the Parts of a Circle

What You Need to Know

The line that forms a circle has no beginning or end; it is a simple closed curve. Any point on the circumference of a circle is the same distance from the center of the circle. A line segment from a point on the circumference of a circle to its center is called the **radius**. Any line segment that begins and ends on the circle's circumference is called a **chord**. A chord that passes through the center of a circle is called the **diameter**.

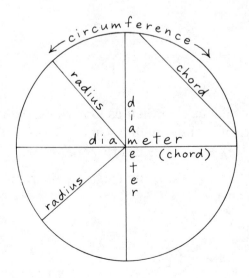

The diameter of any circle is twice as long as the radius of the circle. Every circle has an unlimited number of radii and diameters. For a given circle, all radii are congruent and all diameters are congruent.

Let's Think It Through

Use a compass to draw a circle with a 4-inch (10-cm) diameter.

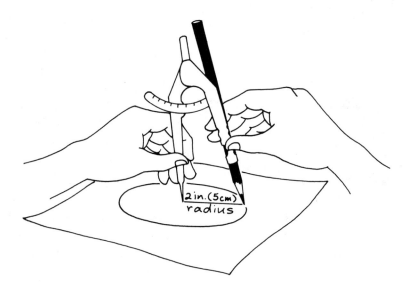

Answer

Think!

- The radius of the circle is half as long as the diameter. What is the radius of a circle with a 4-inch (10-cm) diameter? 4 inches (10 cm) ÷ 2 = 2 inches (5 cm).

- Use a ruler to draw a line the length of the radius, which is 2 inches (5 cm).

- The distance from the point of the compass to the pencil point is equal to the radius of the circle. Place the point of the compass on one end of the line and adjust the position of the pencil so that its point touches the opposite end of the line.

- Draw the circle by holding the compass point steady with one hand and rotating the compass one full turn or 360 degrees with the other hand, as shown in the diagram.

Exercises

1. The diagram shows that Holly and Andrew have worked together to draw a circle in the sand. If the length of rope between the two children is 6 feet (2 m), what is the:

  a. radius of the circle?

  b. diameter of the circle?

2. Use a compass to draw a pie with a radius of 4 inches (10 cm). With a ruler, draw straight lines to divide the pie into eight equal pieces. Study your diagram to answer the following:

  a. What is the diameter of the pie?

  b. How many congruent diameters are shown?

Activity: SPREADERS

Purpose   To produce curved, multicolored patterns.

Materials   one 8-inch (20-cm) coffee filter (basket type)
    drinking glass
    rubber band
    black water-soluble marker
    eyedropper
    tap water
    ruler

Procedure

1. Stretch the coffee filter over the mouth of the glass.

2. Use the rubber band to hold the filter tightly against the glass.

3. Use the black marker to draw a circle with a diameter of about ¼ inch (0.6 cm) in the center of the filter paper.

4. Draw a second circle with a diameter of about ¾ inch (1.9 cm) around the first circle.

5. Use the eyedropper to add one drop of water to the center of the circles.

6. Wait about 10 seconds and add a second drop of water.

7. Continue waiting about 10 seconds and adding one drop of water to the center of the circles until five drops have been added.

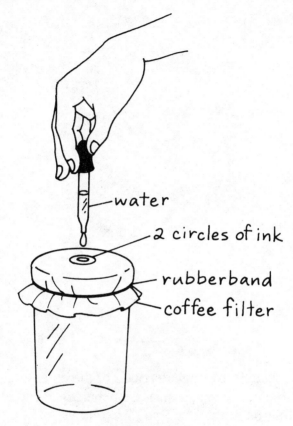

water

2 circles of ink

rubberband

coffee filter

8. Allow the paper to dry. This should take 5 to 10 minutes.

9. Remove the rubber band and spread the paper flat.

10. Use the ruler to measure, in four different places, the diameter of the outer circle produced by the spreading ink.

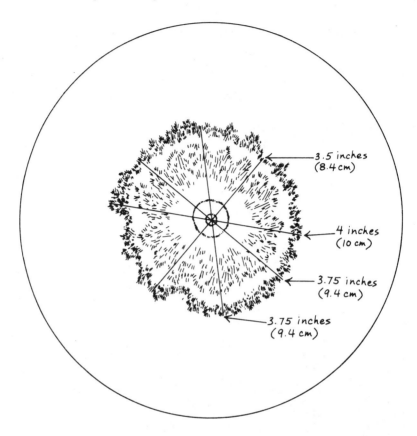

3.5 inches
(8.4 cm)

4 inches
(10 cm)

3.75 inches
(9.4 cm)

3.75 inches
(9.4 cm)

11. Calculate the average diameter of the outer circle by adding the four diameter measurements together and dividing
by four as in the example that follows:

3.5 inches (8.8 cm)
3.75 inches (9.4 cm)
3.75 inches (9.4 cm)
+ 4.00 inches (10.0 cm)
_____
15.00 inches (37.6 cm)

15 inches (37.6 cm) ÷ 4 = 3.75 inches (9.4 cm)

Results A multicolored, jagged-edged, circular figure with
an average diameter of 3.75 inches (9.4 cm) is produced.

Why?   As the water is absorbed by the paper, the black ink dissolves. The black ink is made from a combination of different colors. In water, most black water-soluble ink separates into the three primary colors of yellow, red, and blue. The colors spread outward to different distances depending on the weight of the chemicals and their **affinity** (attraction) to the paper. This results in a multicolored figure that is the general shape of a circle with an irregular line forming its circumference.

Solutions to Exercises

1a. *Think!*

- The rope is stretched from the center to the circumference of the circle. Thus, the length of the rope is equal to the radius of the circle.

The radius is 6 feet (2 m).

b. *Think!*

- The diameter of a circle is twice as long as the circle's radius. Thus, the diameter of the circle is: 2 × 6 feet (2 m).

The diameter is 12 feet (4 m).

2a. *Think!*

- The diameter of a circle is twice as long as the circle's radius. Thus, the diameter of the circular pie is: 2 × 4 inches (10 cm).

The diameter is 8 inches (20 cm).

b. *Think!*

- How many separate 8-inch (20-cm) lines cross the pie when it is divided into eight equal pieces?

There are four congruent diameters.

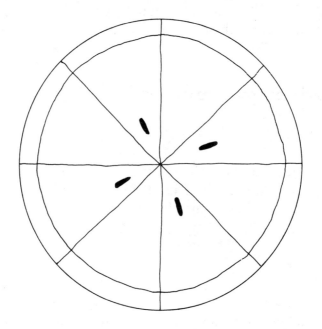

11
Around and Around

Drawing and Measuring Central Angles

What You Need to Know

When the vertex of an angle is at the center of a circle, the angle is called a **central angle**. In the example, angle JAM (∠JAM) is a central angle.

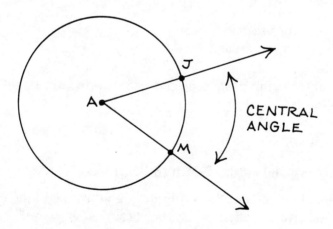

CENTRAL ANGLE

The size of the circle does not alter the size of the angle. The angle between the hands on the small clock is the same as the angle between the hands on the larger clock.

Mathematician's Toolbox: STRING PROTRACTOR

Materials ruler
scissors
string
protractor
transparent tape

Construct a string protractor and use it to measure angles by following these steps:

Procedure

1. Measure and cut a 12-inch (30-cm) piece of string.

2. Thread one end of the string through the hole in the center of the straight edge of the protractor.

3. Tape about 1 inch (2.5 cm) of this end of the string to the back of the protractor.

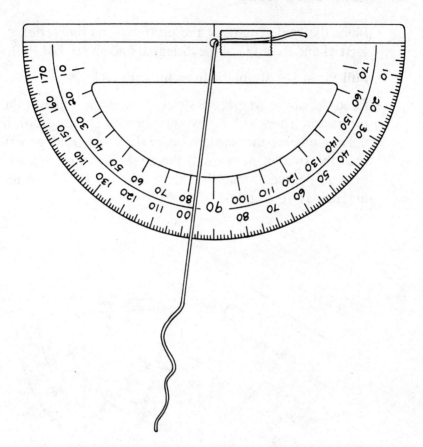

4. Follow these steps to measure the central angle in the
diagram with the string protractor:

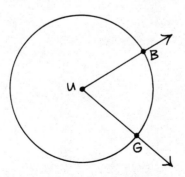

- Place the center mark of the protractor on the vertex of ∠BUG and the edge of the 0-degree line on ray UB (U⃗B.)

- Pull the string so that it lines up with U⃗G.

- Read the angle where the string crosses the scale of the protractor. There will be two numbers to choose from. If the angle being measured is acute (less than 90 degrees), read the smaller number. If the angle is obtuse (greater than 90 degrees), read the larger number. ∠BUG in the diagram is 70 degrees.

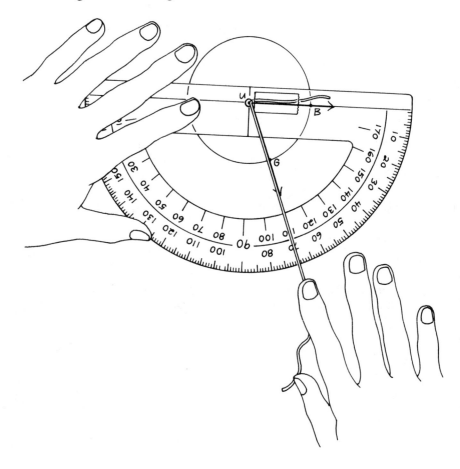

Let's Think It Through

Use your string protractor to measure the central angle, angle SEA, between the second and sixth spokes on the ship's steering wheel.

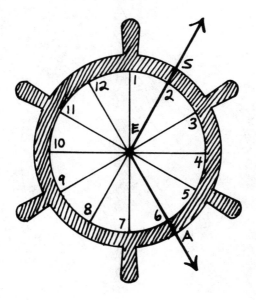

Answer

Think!

- Place the center mark of the protractor on the vertex of ∠SEA and the edge of the 0-degree line on $\overrightarrow{ES}$.

- Pull the string so that it lines up with $\overrightarrow{EA}$.

- Is ∠SEA acute or obtuse? Obtuse.

• Which of the angle choices under the string is obtuse? ∠*SEA is 120 degrees.*

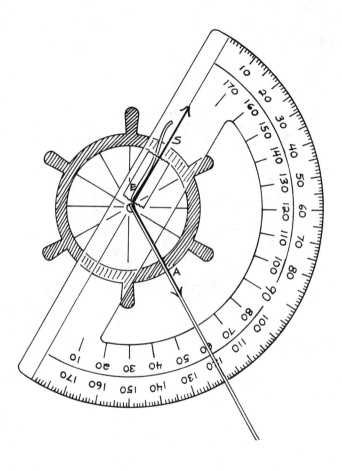

Exercise

How many degrees must the ship turn to be on a course headed directly toward the island?

Activity: 12 O'CLOCK HIGH

Purpose To use the hands of a clock to estimate direction.

Materials typing paper
pencil
scissors
paper plate
paper fastener
adult helper

Procedure

1. Lay the typing paper over the pattern of the clock hands and trace them with the pencil.

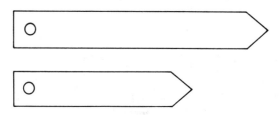

2. Cut out the traced clock hands.

3. Ask your adult helper to use the point of the pencil to punch a hole in the center of the paper plate and through the circle on each clock hand.

4. Use the paper fastener to attach the hands in the center of the plate. Place the shorter hand on top.

5. Write the numbers 1 through 12 around the edge of the paper plate as they would appear on the face of a clock.

6. Imagine that you and a friend are standing side by side, studying the stars in the sky. Your friend gives the following locations for two stars:

- Star 1 is at 12 o'clock high.

- Star 2 is to the right at 2 o'clock.

7. Find the approximate location of the stars in the sky by following these steps:

- Hold the paper plate vertically in front of you.

- First, move the hands of the clock to 12 o'clock and observe the direction the hands point, noting the size of the angle, if any, between the hands.

- Leaving the longer hand at 12 o'clock, place the shorter hand at 2 o'clock and again note the size of the angle.

Results   At 12 o'clock high the hands point straight up with no angle between the hands. At 2 o'clock the hands should be 60 degrees apart. Follow the short hand as you look up at the imaginary stars, and you'll see the same thing your friend sees at 2 o'clock.

Why?   When both clock hands are pointing to 12 o'clock, the hands point straight up with no angle between the hands.

"12 o'clock high" is used to instruct a person to look at an object directly overhead. Placing the larger clock hand on 12 and moving the smaller hand to any other number on the clock's face creates an angle between the two hands.

The face of a clock is a circle, and like any other circle it measures 360 degrees around. The numbers on the clock break the 360 degrees into 12 even parts. The number of degrees between each number on the clock can be calculated by dividing 360 degrees by 12, which is 30 degrees. This means that the angle between the clock hands placed on consecutive numbers on the clock, such as on 12 and 1, is 30 degrees. At 2 o'clock the clock hands are two numbers apart, making the angle 2 × 30 degrees, or 60 degrees.

The star at position 2 o'clock in the sky is found by looking straight up and moving your eyes to view a spot overhead about 60 degrees to the right of where you are facing.

Solution to Exercise

Think!

- Measure ∠RIG with your protractor.
- Is the angle acute or obtuse? Acute.
- Which of the angle choices under the string is acute? 60 degrees.

The boat would have to turn 60 degrees.

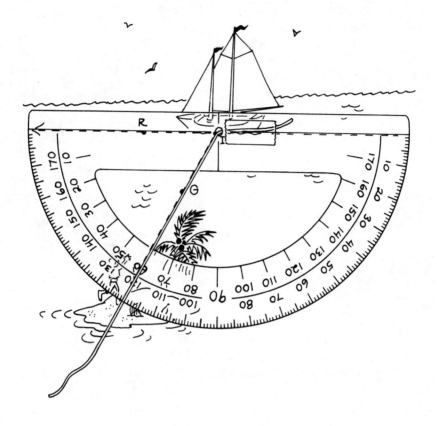

12
Too Odd
Tracing Plane Geometric Figures

What You Need to Know

Some plane figures can be traced with one continuous stroke of a pencil and others cannot. When doing this, the pencil is not lifted from the paper and no line is traced twice. The clue to determining which figures can be traced with this method is the number of line segments that meet at each vertex. If a figure has an even number of line segments meeting at each vertex, as in figures A and B, you can start at any vertex and trace every line segment in the figure only once with one continuous stroke.

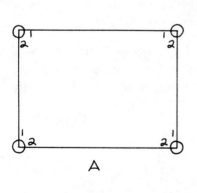

A

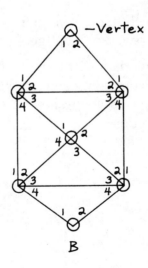

—Vertex

B

Some figures have vertices in which an odd number of line segments meet. Figures with only two vertices at which an odd number of line segments meet can be traced with one continuous stroke, but you must start at one of the odd vertices and finish at the other odd vertex. If the figure has more than two odd vertices, it cannot be drawn without lifting the pencil.

Let's Think It Through

Look at figures C and D to answer the following:

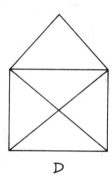

C   D

1. Which figure can be traced with one continuous stroke of the pencil without going over the same line twice?

2. Draw on a sheet of paper the figure(s) that can be traced with one continuous stroke. Use an *S* to indicate the starting point, an *E* to show the endpoint, and arrows to show direction.

Answers

1. *Think!*

- Are there more than two odd vertices in either figure?
  Yes, figure C has four odd vertices, at vertices 1, 2, 3, and
  4. Figure C cannot be traced without lifting the pencil.

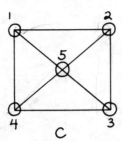

- How many odd vertices does figure D have? Two, at
  vertices 3 and 4.

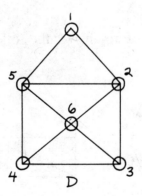

*Figure D can be drawn with one continuous stroke of the
pencil.*

2. *Think!*

- Because it has two odd vertices, figure D can be traced with one continuous stroke if the starting point S is at one of the odd vertices, 3 or 4, and the endpoint E is at the other odd vertex. One of the two possible routes is shown here.

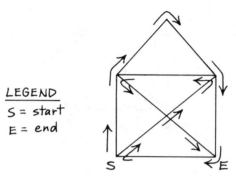

LEGEND
S = start
E = end

Exercises

Study figures E and F to answer the following:

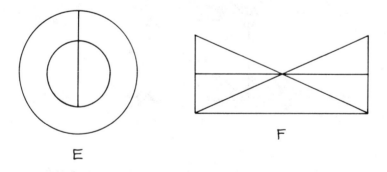

E

F

1. Determine which figure(s) can be traced with one continuous stroke without going over the same line twice.

2. Draw on a sheet of paper the figure(s) that can be traced with one continuous stroke. Use an *S* to indicate the starting point, an *E* to show the endpoint, and arrows to show direction.

Activity: IMPOSSIBLE CHALLENGE

Purpose To draw a circle within a circle in one continuous stroke of a pencil.

Materials pencil
paper
helper

Procedure

1. Challenge a helper to draw a circle within a circle without lifting the pencil from the paper.

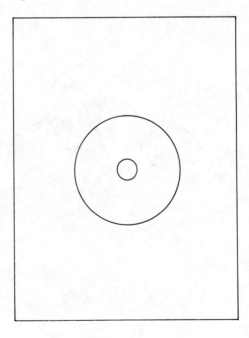

2. When your helper has given up, follow the steps below to show that you can successfully perform this seemingly impossible challenge:

- Fold the paper so that the top right corner is in the middle of the paper.

- Draw a small circle on the front of the paper, beginning at the tip of the folded corner.

- From this circle, draw a straight line about 2 inches (5 cm) long on the back of the folded corner.

- Without lifting the pencil, begin to draw a large circle on the back of the paper, moving the pencil counterclockwise. Do not stop when you reach the edge of the folded corner.

- Continue drawing the large circle on the front of the paper, stopping when you reach the other edge of the folded corner.

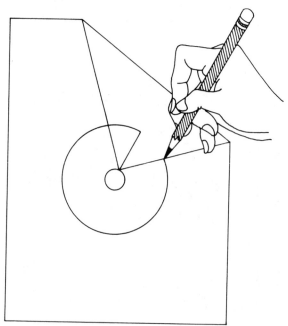

- Hold the pencil in place while you lift the folded corner.
- Finish the circle.

Results   A circle within a circle is drawn with one continuous stroke of the pencil.

Why?   The folded corner of the paper provides a bridge between the inner and outer circles. Once the corner is lifted, the straight line drawn on the back of the paper is not visible on the front of the paper.

Solutions to Exercises

1. *Think!*

- How many odd vertices does each figure have? Figure E has two, at vertices 1 and 3. Figure F has four, at vertices 2, 3, 6, and 7.

- Figures with two odd vertices can be traced with one continuous stroke, but figures with more than two cannot be traced without lifting the pencil.

Figure E can be traced with one continuous stroke.

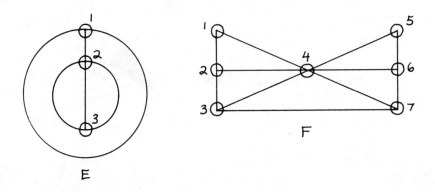

2. *Think!*

- Because it has two odd vertices, figure E can be traced with one continuous stroke if the starting point S is at one of the odd vertices, 1 or 3, and the endpoint E is at the other odd vertex. The following is one of the two possible solutions.

LEGEND

S = start

E = end

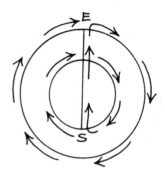

13

Reverse Copy

Determining Lines of Symmetry in Geometric Figures

What You Need to Know

A **line of symmetry** divides a figure into two identical parts that are mirror images of each other, meaning, if a mirror is placed on the line of the folded figure, the whole figure can be seen. If the figure is folded along the line of symmetry, the two halves will exactly match.

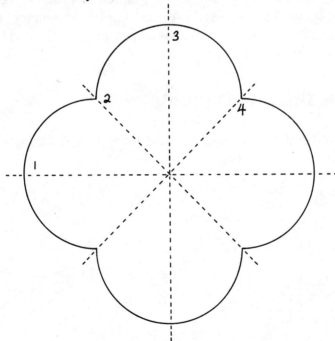

Figures with lines of symmetry are called **symmetric figures**. Some symmetric figures have one line of symmetry, while others have more than one line of symmetry, as indicated by the diagrams on pages 103 and 104.

Let's Think It Through

Determine if the dotted lines are lines of symmetry for the figures on the next page.

1.

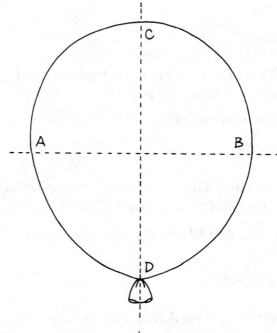

2.

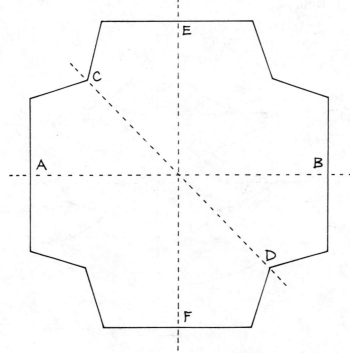

Answers

1. Think!

- On which line(s) can the figure be folded to form two halves that exactly match?

$\overleftrightarrow{CD}$ *is a line of symmetry.*

2. Think!

- On which line(s) can the figure be folded to form two halves that exactly match?

$\overleftrightarrow{AB}$, $\overleftrightarrow{CD}$, *and* $\overleftrightarrow{EF}$ *are all lines of symmetry.*

Exercises

1. Determine if the dotted lines are lines of symmetry for the figures.

a.

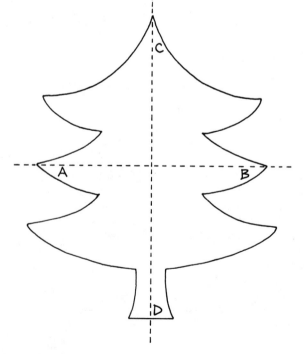

b.

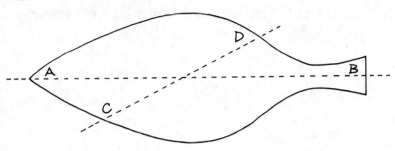

c.

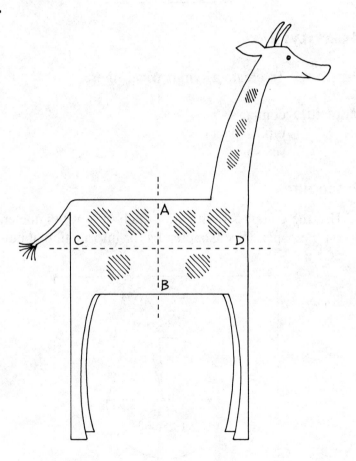

2. Trace the equilateral triangle on paper and cut it out. Fold the cutout to determine how many lines of symmetry the triangle has.

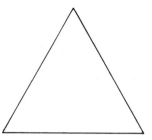

Activity: LACY

Purpose To create a symmetrical figure.

Materials compass
          typing paper
          scissors

Procedure

1. Use the compass to draw a 4-inch (10-cm) diameter circle on the paper. (See Chapter 10 for information about diameter.)

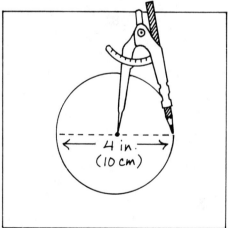

2. Cut out the circle.

3. Fold the circle in half three times.

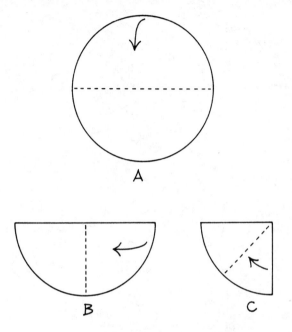

4. Cut four triangular notches in each side and one at the pointed end of the folded paper.

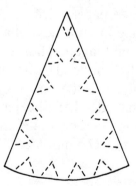

5. Unfold the paper.

Results   A lacy pattern is produced.

Why?   Folding the paper three times produces eight layers of paper. The triangular notches cut along the edges are cut
through each of the eight layers. Thus, the design repeats eight
times around the entire circle. The notches cut on the curved
edge remain triangular, but the notches cut on a folded edge
become diamond shaped when the paper is unfolded. The
notch cut at the pointed end becomes an eight-pointed star in
the middle of the figure. The unfolded figure has four lines of
symmetry.

Solutions to Exercises

1a. *Think!*

> • On which line(s) can the figure be folded to form two halves that exactly match?

$\overleftrightarrow{CD}$ *is a line of symmetry.*

b. *Think!*

> • On which line(s) can the figure be folded to form two halves that exactly match?

$\overleftrightarrow{AB}$ *is a line of symmetry.*

c. *Think!*

> • On which line(s) can the figure be folded to form two halves that exactly match?

None of the lines are lines of symmetry.

2. *Think!*

> • On how many lines can the paper be folded to form two halves that exactly match?

The equilateral triangle has three lines of symmetry.

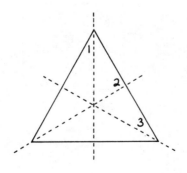

14
Plane Art
Using Plane Geometry to Make Artistic Designs

What You Need to Know

The figures and shapes of plane geometry have been used for centuries to decorate everything from Egyptian pottery and American Indian blankets to modern wallpaper and gift-wrapping paper. In this chapter you will create geometrical art by using line segments to connect numbered points on a plane figure. All of the experiments are based on metric measurements. If you prefer, you may substitute whole inches for centimeters, but you will need to use larger paper.

Let's Think It Through

Use the following steps to draw a curved design by connecting points on an angle:

1. Use a metric ruler and a protractor to draw two 6-cm lines at right angles to each other. Make a dot and number each centimeter division on each ray of the angle as shown in the diagram on the next page.

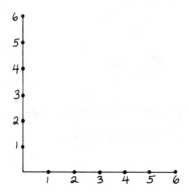

2. Using the edge of the ruler, draw a line segment to connect points on one ray to points on the other ray. Connect the points on **adjacent** (adjoining or neighboring) rays in this way: 1 to 6, 2 to 5, 3 to 4, and so on.

Answer

Think!

- A right angle that has congruent rays is symmetrical, so the curve created by connecting the points on adjacent rays is also symmetrical.

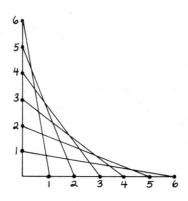

Exercises

Use the steps in Let's Think It Through to draw curved designs that have the following angles and ray lengths. Determine how the shape of the curve changes in each drawing.

1. Draw a 140-degree (obtuse) angle, each ray of which is 6 cm long. Divide the rays into six equal parts as shown in the diagram, then create the curve.

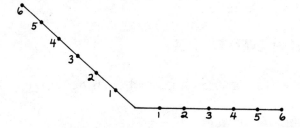

2. Draw a right angle measuring 3 cm along one ray and 6 cm along the other. Divide both rays into six equal parts as shown in the diagram, then create the curve.

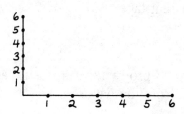

3. Draw a 30-degree (acute) angle, each ray of which is 6 cm long. Divide the rays into six equal parts as shown in the diagram, then create the curve.

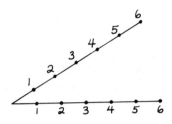

Activity: STITCHERY

Purpose   To construct a geometric string design.

Materials   metric ruler
protractor
scissors
typing paper
marking pen
pencil with eraser
colored sewing thread
sewing needle
transparent tape

Procedure

1. Use the ruler and protractor to measure and cut a 15-by-15 cm square from the paper.

2. With the pen, draw a 10-by-10-cm square in the center of the paper.

3. Use dots to divide each side into 20 $\frac{1}{2}$-cm parts and number each dot with the pen, as shown in the diagram. This will be called the back side of the paper.

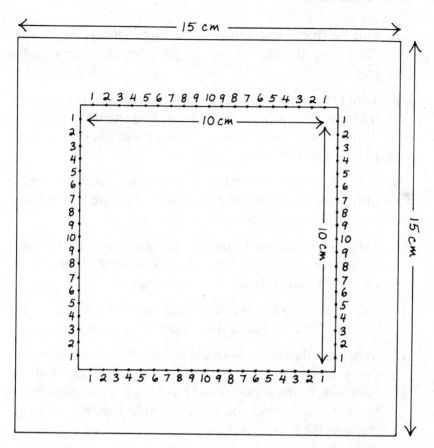

4. During the daytime, turn the paper over so the front side faces you, and place it against a windowpane. The light from outside will allow you to see the marks through the paper. With a pencil, lightly mark and number each division.

5. Thread the needle with about 2 feet (60 cm) of thread. Pull the thread through the eye of the needle so that the two ends meet. Tie a knot in the two ends.

6. Starting on the back side of the paper, begin working in one angle of the square. Insert the needle through one of the points numbered 1.

7. Pull the thread through until the knot in the string touches the paper. Be careful not to pull the knot through the paper.

8. Turn the paper over and on the front side insert the needle into point 10 on the adjacent ray. Pull the thread through the hole in the paper until it creates a straight line between points 1 and 10.

9. Turn the paper over and on the back side insert the needle into point 9 on the same ray. Pull the thread through and across to point 2 on the previous ray.

10. Continue this process until all the points in the first angle have been connected. You will end at point 10 on the ray on which you started.

11. Repeat steps 6 to 10 in the adjacent angle, and continue until all four angles of the square have been connected.

12. When the thread starts to get too short to reach from one point to another, cut it off about 1 inch (2.5 cm) from the back side of the paper. When the design is complete, twist the hanging threads on the back side together and tape them to the paper.

13. Carefully erase the pencil marks on the front side.

Results   The design shown on the next page is created by the colored thread on the front side of the paper.

Why?   As in the diagram made earlier in the Let's Think It Through section, in which line segments were drawn between the points on the rays of a right angle, the colored thread creates a line segment between the points on the stitched design. Try creating and stitching your own geometric designs.

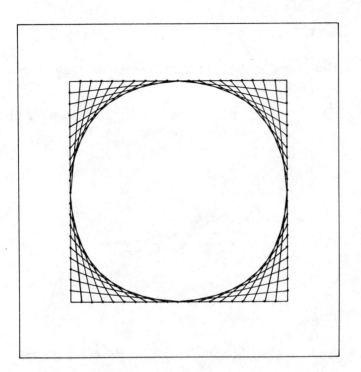

Solutions to Exercises

1. *Think!*

- Both rays are the same length and the angle is obtuse.
- The curve is symmetrical and very slight.

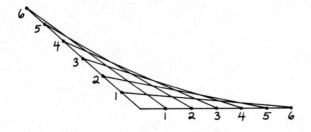

2. *Think!*

- Both rays are not the same length, so the curve is not symmetrical.

- The right angle produces a greater curve than the obtuse angle in the previous example.

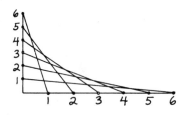

3. *Think!*

- Both rays are the same length, so the curve is symmetrical.

- As angles get smaller, the curves become more pointed. This figure has the smallest angle and the most pointed curve.

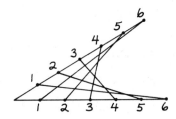

15

What's Next?

Extending and Relating Geometric Patterns

What You Need to Know

A **pattern** is a predictable arrangement of things, such as numbers and/or geometric figures, that have some relationship to each other. To solve a problem, it is sometimes necessary to see if a pattern exists in the problem. In this chapter only geometric figures will be used to create and extend patterns. These figures may vary in size, shape, color, or position, but they work together to form a pattern that can be recognized and extended. An example of predicting the extension of a geometric pattern is shown in the diagram. A large colorless geometric figure is followed by a smaller dark figure of the same geometric shape. The most logical prediction of the next figure would be a smaller dark circle.

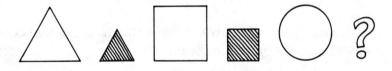

Let's Think It Through

What would be the next figure in each pattern?

1.

2.

Answers

1. *Think!*

- What figures are shown in the problem? Ice cream cones with one scoop of ice cream.

- How do the figures differ? There are two different flavors of ice cream.

- What is the pattern? The flavor of the ice cream in the cones alternates.

• The next ice cream cone would be:

2. *Think!*

• What figures are shown in the pattern? Smiley faces.

• How do the figures differ? They vary in size; also the small faces have legs and feet and the large faces wear hats.

• What is the pattern? The size of the faces alternates.

• The next figure would be:

Exercises

What would be the next figure in each pattern?

1.

2.

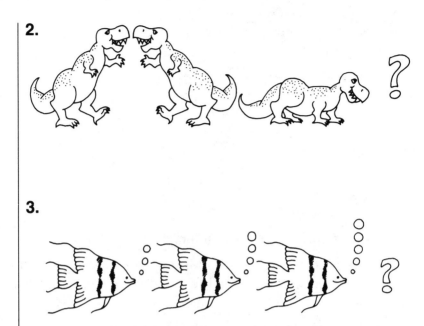

3.

Activity: BOUNCER

Purpose To demonstrate a repeated pattern.

Materials ruler
scissors
typing paper
marking pen
transparent tape

Procedure

1. Measure and cut two strips of paper that are 2 × 4 inches (5 × 10 cm).

2. Draw a line across the shorter side of the paper strips 1 inch (2.5 cm) from each end.

3. Tape the top and bottom of one strip to a table.

4. Starting on the bottom line of the taped strip, draw a stick figure about 1 inch (2.5 cm) tall that has both arms down and a ball resting on the bottom line.

5. Place the second paper strip on top of the drawing with the edges of the strips lined up, and tape the top of this strip to the table.

6. Trace the figure onto the top paper, but raise one arm and place the ball in the stick figure's hand.

7. Tape a pencil to the bottom edge of the top paper as shown.

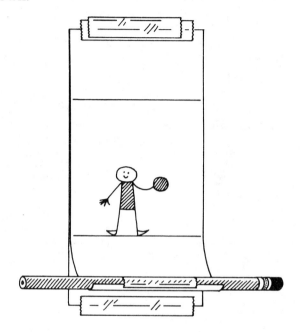

8. Place your hands on the ends of the pencil and roll the pencil up to the top line drawn on the paper.

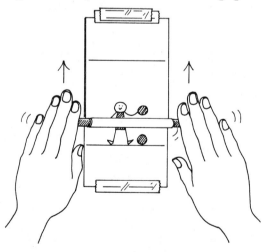

9. Quickly roll the pencil back and forth between the two lines on the paper several times.

Results   The ball appears to bounce up and down.

Why?   The human eye retains an image of an object for a fraction of a second after the object is out of sight. This retention of an image is called **persistence of vision**. When two related images are quickly flashed one after the other, the brain combines the images and perceives that the images are in motion. Rolling the top paper strip back and forth allows one picture to follow the other so quickly that persistence of vision lasts long enough to bridge the time between one image and the next. This creates the illusion that the ball is bouncing up and down.

Solutions to Exercises

1. *Think!*

- What figures are shown? Clown heads.
- How do the figures differ? The heads are facing different directions.
- What is the pattern? The direction of the heads alternates.
- The next figure would be:

2. *Think!*

- What figures are shown? Cartoon dinosaurs.

- How do the figures differ? The dinosaur's body is in different positions.

- What is the pattern? Each dinosaur is in a different position, but the position of the second dinosaur is a mirror image of the first dinosaur. The fourth dinosaur must therefore be a mirror image of the third dinosaur.

- The next figure would be:

3. *Think!*

- What figures are shown? Fish blowing bubbles.

- How do the figures differ? The number and size of the bubbles are different.

- What is the pattern? The next fish in line has one extra bubble that is larger than the largest bubble of the preceding fish.

- The next figure would be:

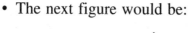

16
Coverup

Calculating the Area of a Rectangle

What You Need to Know

A plane figure is **two-dimensional** because its surface can be measured in only two directions—length and width. **Area** is the measure of the number of square units needed to cover this surface. This chapter deals with the area of rectangles. To calculate the area of a rectangle, use the formula A = l × w, which is read: area equals length times width.

Let's Think It Through

What is the area of the rectangle shown?

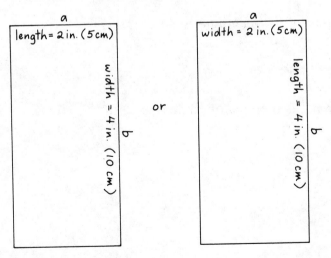

or

Answer

Think!

- The formula for calculating the area of a rectangle is
  $A = l \times w$.

- Sides a and b of the diagram may be labeled as either the length or the width without changing the results.

- When two units are multiplied, such as in. $\times$ in., a small 2 is placed to the upper right of the unit: in.^{2}. This is read: square inches (cm $\times$ cm = cm^2; and is read: square centimeters).

- The area of the rectangle is:

• **English**	**Metric**
$A = l \times w$	$A = l \times w$
$= 2$ in. $\times 4$ in.	$= 5$ cm $\times 10$ cm
$= 8$ in.^{2}	$= 50$ cm^2
or	or
$A = 4$ in. $\times 2$ in.	$A = 10$ cm $\times 5$ cm
$= 8$ in.^{2}	$= 50$ cm^2

The area of the rectangle is 8 in.^{2} (50 cm^2).

Exercises

1. What is the area of Katherine's scarf?

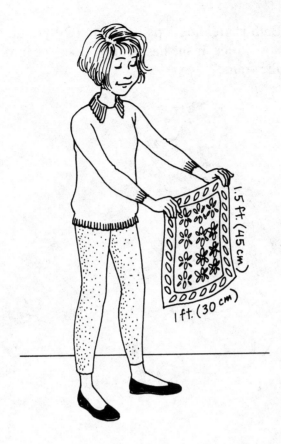

2. Marlin mows his lawn twice a month. What is the total area that he mows each month?

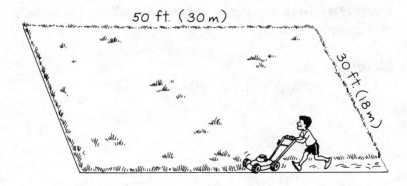

3. Anna Beth is creating a picture using 2-by-2-in. (5-by-5-cm) colored tiles. If she has 60 tiles, does she have enough to fill the frame?

Activity: TWIRLER STICK

Purpose   To determine if surface area affects the movement of a spinning object.

Material   ruler
new pencil with eraser
small handsaw
scissors
index card
pushpin
round pen
adult helper

Procedure

1. Ask your adult helper to make a twirler stick by following these steps:

   - Starting about 1½ inches (3.8 cm) from the end of the pencil eraser, use the saw to cut notches as close together as possible on one side of the pencil for the next 4 inches (10 cm).

   - Measure and cut from the index card two rectangular propellers: a small one ½ × 2 inches (1.25 × 5 cm) and a larger one 2 × 2 inches (5 × 5 cm).

   - Push the pushpin through the center of the small propeller. Move the pushpin around to enlarge the hole in the paper so that the propeller spins freely on the pushpin.

   - Repeat the previous step to prepare the hole in the large propeller.

   - Place the pushpin through the hole in the small propeller, and attach the propeller to the twirler stick by sticking the pushpin in the end of the eraser.

2. Hold the twirler stick in one hand and a round pen in the other hand with your index finger on the nonwriting end of the pen.

3. Rub the round pen back and forth across the notches while rubbing your index finger against the side of the pencil.

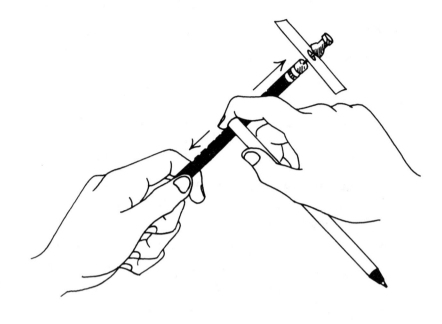

4. Ask your adult helper to take off the small propeller and put on the large propeller.

5. Repeat steps 2 and 3.

Results Both propellers turn, but the smaller one is usually easier to get started.

Why? The pen bumps and hits as it is rubbed across the notches, causing the pencil to vibrate. Moving your finger results in a curved vibrational motion, causing the propeller to spin. The larger propeller has more surface area to be affected by this movement, so it takes more energy to get it started.

Solutions to Exercises

1. *Think!*

- The formula for calculating the area of the scarf is:

  - **English**   **Metric**

    $A = l \times w$ $A = l \times w$
    $\quad = 1 \text{ ft.} \times 1.5 \text{ ft.}$ $\quad = 30 \text{ cm} \times 45 \text{ cm}$
    $\quad = 1.5 \text{ ft.}^2$ $\quad = 1{,}350 \text{ cm}^2$

The area of Katherine's scarf is 1.5 ft.² (1,350 cm²).

2. *Think!*

- The formula for calculating the area of the lawn is:

  - **English**   **Metric**

    $A = l \times w$ $A = l \times w$
    $\quad = 50 \text{ ft.} \times 30 \text{ ft.}$ $\quad = 30 \text{ m} \times 18 \text{ m}$
    $\quad = 1{,}500 \text{ ft.}^2$ $\quad = 540 \text{ m}^2$

- Mowing the lawn twice a month means that Marlin covers two times the surface area of the lawn: $2 \times 1{,}500$ ft.² (540 m²).

Marlin mows 3,000 ft.² (1,080 m²) each month.

3. *Think!*

- The area of each tile is:

  - **English**   **Metric**

    $A = l \times w$ $A = l \times w$
    $\quad = 2 \text{ in.} \times 2 \text{ in.}$ $\quad = 5 \text{ cm} \times 5 \text{ cm}$
    $\quad = 4 \text{ in.}^2$ $\quad = 25 \text{ cm}^2$

- The area inside the picture frame is:

  - **English**   **Metric**

    $A = l \times w$ $A = l \times w$
    $\quad = 10 \text{ in.} \times 20 \text{ in.}$ $\quad = 25 \text{ cm} \times 50 \text{ cm}$
    $\quad = 200 \text{ in.}^2$ $\quad = 1{,}250 \text{ cm}^2$

- Determine the number of tiles needed by dividing the area inside the frame by the area of one tile.

  - **English**   **Metric**

    $200 \text{ in.}^2 \div 4 \text{ in.}^2 = 50$ $1{,}250 \text{ cm}^2 \div 25 \text{ cm}^2 = 50$

- 50 tiles are needed.

Yes, Anna Beth has enough tiles.

17
Same Size

Calculating the Area
of a Rhomboid or Rhombus

What You Need to Know

As explained in Chapter 5, a rhomboid (also called a parallelo-gram) and a rhombus have no right angles. The opposite sides of a rhomboid are parallel, and only its opposite sides are congruent. The opposite sides of a rhombus are parallel, and all four sides are congruent.

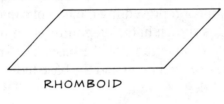

RHOMBOID

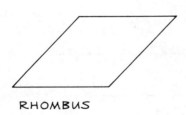

RHOMBUS

The terms *base* and *height* are used when measuring triangles, rhombuses, and rhomboids. (The terms *length* and *width* are used to describe the same measurements on squares and rectangles.) The formula for calculating the area of a rhomboid or rhombus is: $A = b \times h$, which is read: area equals base times height.

Any side of the rhomboid or rhombus may be labeled as the base (b), but it is customary to label the bottom horizontal line as the base as shown in the diagram. This method will be used in this chapter.

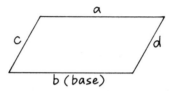

The height of a rhomboid or rhombus is measured by drawing a perpendicular line between the base and its opposite, parallel side. The line must form a right (90-degree) angle with the base. The line segment representing the height can be drawn in various positions as shown in the diagrams, but it must always be at a right angle (90 degrees) to the base. The small square drawn at the vertex of the height and the base indicates that the lines meet at a 90-degree angle.

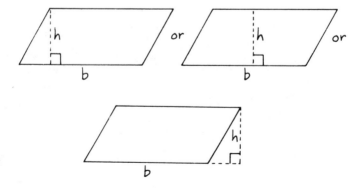

Let's Think It Through

Find the area of the rhomboid shown.

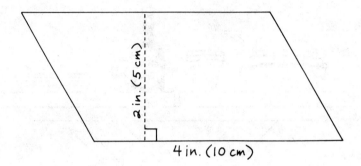

Answer

Think!

* The formula for calculating the area of a rhomboid is
  $A = b \times h$.
* The base (the bottom horizontal line) measures 4 inches (10 cm).
* The height (the line drawn between the base and its opposite parallel side) is 2 inches (5 cm).

English	**Metric**
$A = b \times h$	$A = b \times h$
$= 4 \text{ in.} \times 2 \text{ in.}$	$= 10 \text{ cm} \times 5 \text{ cm}$
$= 8 \text{ in.}^2$	$= 50 \text{ cm}^2$

The area of the rhomboid is 8 in.² (50 cm²).

Exercises

1. Calculate the area of the table leg.

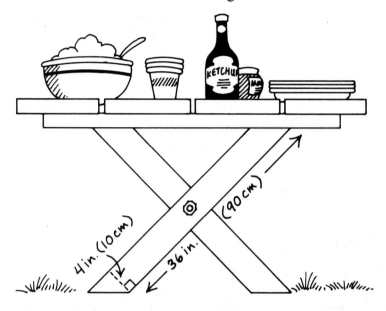

2. Calculate the area of the missing rhombus-shaped puzzle piece in the illustration on the next page.

Activity: HOW HIGH?

Purpose To demonstrate how the height of a rhomboid is determined.

Materials pencil
ruler
index card
scissors

Procedure

1. Use the pencil and ruler to mark two dots on the index card. Make one dot 1½ inches (3.8 cm) from the upper left corner of the card, and the second dot 1 ¹/₂ inches (3.8 cm) from the lower right corner.

2. With a ruler, draw two dashed lines across the card, connecting the dots to the corners on the card as shown on the diagram.

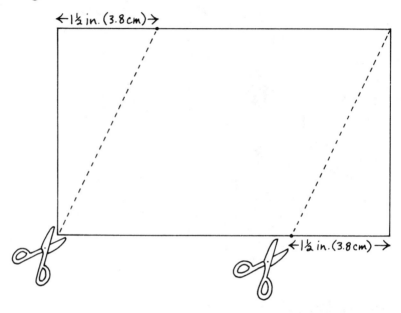

3. Cut along the dashed lines. Keep the rhomboid but discard the triangles.

4. Lay the ruler on top of the rhomboid with the left corner and short edge of the ruler lined up with the left corner and long edge of the rhomboid.

5. Draw a dashed line on the rhomboid along both sides of the ruler.

6. Measure and compare the length of each of the two dashed lines.

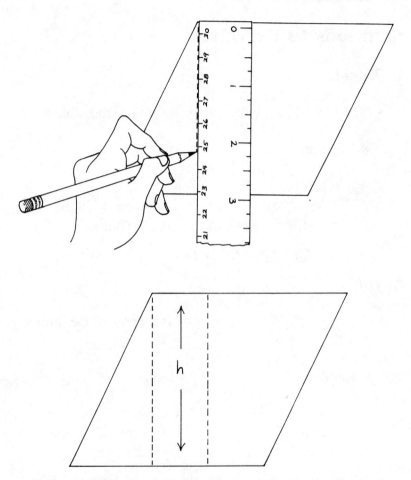

Results   The length of both lines is equal.

Why?   The dimensions of a rhomboid are called the base and height. The height is the perpendicular distance between the base and its parallel side. Thus, as shown in this activity, all perpendicular lines drawn between the base and its parallel side are congruent.

Solutions to Exercises

1. *Think!*

- The formula for calculating the area of the table leg is:

  - **English**   **Metric**

    A = b × h   A = b × h
      = 36 in. × 4 in.   = 90 cm × 10 cm
      = 144 in.²   = 900 cm²

The area of the table leg is 144 in.² (900 cm²).

2. *Think!*

- The formula for calculating the area of the missing puzzle piece is:

  - **English**   **Metric**

    A = b × h   A = b × h
      = 2 in. × 1 in.   = 5 cm × 2.5 cm
      = 2 in.²   = 12.5 cm²

The area of the missing puzzle piece is 2 in.² (12.5 cm²).

18
Pie?

Calculating the Area of a Circle

What You Need to Know

The ratio of the circumference of any circle to its diameter is shown by the value **pi** (π). To calculate the area of a circle, use the formula $A = \pi r^2$, which is read: area equals pi times the square radius, or area equals pi times the radius times the radius.

The value of π is about $3\frac{1}{7}$, but there is no exact number equal to this ratio. Calculators give the most accurate value of this number, but 3.14 is the most common value used and it is the number that is used in this book. Using 3.14 as the value for π, the formula can be written more simply as:

area = $3.14 \times r \times r$.

Let's Think It Through

What is the surface area of the pizza?

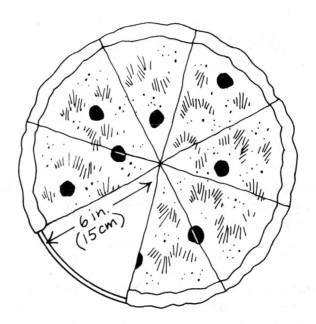

6 in.
(15 cm)

Answer

Think!

- The formula for calculating the area of the pizza is

  A = 3.14 × r × r.

- When multiplying three numbers together, work with two numbers at a time. Multiply the first two, then multiply the product of these two numbers by the third number.

  - **English**

$$A = 3.14 × 6 \text{ in.} × 6 \text{ in.}$$
$$3.14 × 6 \text{ in.} = 18.84 \text{ in.}$$
$$A = 18.84 \text{ in.} × 6 \text{ in.} = 113.04 \text{ in.}^2$$

• **Metric**

$$A = 3.14 \times 15 \text{ cm} \times 15 \text{ cm}$$
$$3.14 \times 15 \text{ cm} = 47.1 \text{ cm}$$
$$A = 47.1 \text{ cm} \times 15 \text{ cm} = 706.5 \text{ cm}^2$$

The area of the pizza is 113.04 in.² (706.5 cm²).

Exercises

1. Determine the area of the lid on the jam jar.

2. The length of each fan blade from the center of the fan is 4 inches (10 cm). Calculate the area of the circle that the blades sweep with each complete turn.

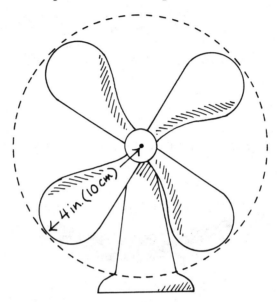

3. Each small square in the diagram has a measurement of 2 × 2 inches (5 × 5 cm). What is the area of the circle?

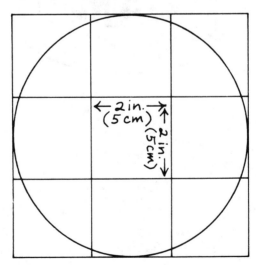

Activity: ROUND OR RECTANGULAR?

Purpose   To compare the area of a rectangle made from parts of a circle with the area of the original circle.

Materials   compass
              typing paper
              pencil
              scissors
              string
              transparent tape

Procedure

1. Use the compass to draw a circle with a 4-inch (10-cm) radius on the paper.

2. Lay the paper over the diagram with the center of the circle over the vertex of the rays.

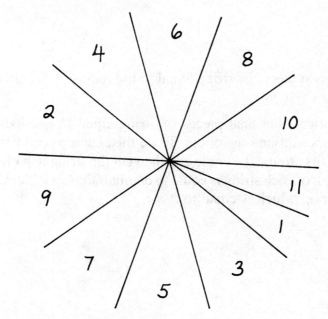

3. Trace each ray, extending it to the circumference of the circle.

4. Number each section in the circle as shown.

5. Use the pencil to shade the bottom half of the circle.

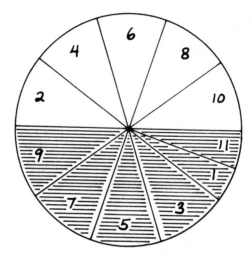

6. Cut two pieces of string equal to the radius of the circle, 4 inches (10 cm).

7. Cut two additional pieces of string equal to one-half the distance around the circle. To do this, cut a piece of string that fits around the circle and then cut the string in half. The length of each string is equal to one-half the circle's circumference, which is equal to $\pi \times r$.

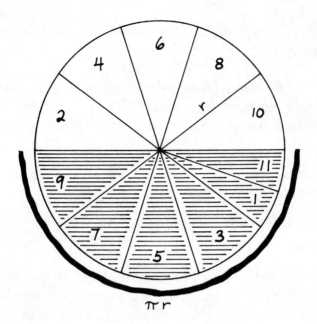

8. Tape the ends of the strings to a table so that they form a rectangle.

9. Cut out the pie-shaped pieces from the circle and arrange them inside the rectangle made by the string, as shown in the diagram.

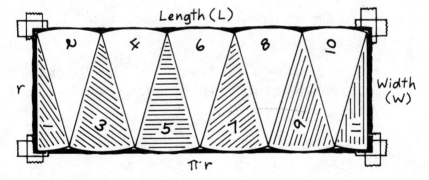

Results   The pieces from the circle fit almost exactly into a rectangular shape.

Why?   The formulas for calculating the area of a rectangle and that of a circle can be compared. The formula for calculating the area of the rectangle made from the pieces of the circle is:

$$A = l \times w$$
$$= \pi \times r \times r$$

The formula for calculating the area of the circle is:

$$A = \pi \times r^2$$

While the formulas for calculating the areas of the rectangle and the circle are the same, the areas are only approximately equal because the pie pieces do not fit exactly into the rectangle.

Solutions to Exercises

1. *Think!*

- The formula for calculating the area of the lid is

  $A = 3.14 \times r \times r.$

- If the diameter is 4 inches (10 cm), then the radius is one-half this measurement: $\frac{1}{2} \times 4$ in. (10 cm) = 2 in. (5 cm).

  - **English**

$$A = 3.14 \times 2 \text{ in.} \times 2 \text{ in.}$$
$$3.14 \times 2 \text{ in.} = 6.28 \text{ in.}$$
$$A = 6.28 \text{ in.} \times 2 \text{ in.}$$
$$= 12.56 \text{ in.}^2$$

- **Metric**

$$A = 3.14 \times 5 \text{ cm} \times 5 \text{ cm}$$
$$3.14 \times 5 \text{ cm} = 15.7 \text{ cm}$$
$$A = 15.7 \text{ cm} \times 5 \text{ cm}$$
$$= 78.5 \text{ cm}^2$$

The area of the lid on the jam jar is 12.56 in.² (78.5 cm²).

2. Think!

- The formula for calculating the area of the circle is
  $A = 3.14 \times r \times r$.
- The length of the fan blade is equal to the radius of the fan.

  - **English**

$$A = 3.14 \times 4 \text{ in.} \times 4 \text{ in.}$$
$$3.14 \times 4 \text{ in.} = 12.56 \text{ in.}$$
$$A = 12.56 \text{ in.} \times 4 \text{ in.}$$
$$= 50.24 \text{ in.}^2$$

  - **Metric**

$$A = 3.14 \times 10 \text{ cm} \times 10 \text{ cm}$$
$$3.14 \times 10 \text{ cm} = 31.40 \text{ cm}$$
$$A = 31.40 \text{ cm} \times 10 \text{ cm}$$
$$= 314.0 \text{ cm}^2$$

The area of the circle that the fan blades sweep with each complete turn is 50.24 in.² (314.0 cm²).

3. *Think!*

- The diameter of the circle is equal to three times the width of one small square: 3×2 in. (5 cm) = 6 in. (15 cm).

- If the diameter is 6 inches (15 cm), then the radius is one-half this measurement: $\frac{1}{2} \times 6$ in. (15 cm) = 3 in. (7.5 cm).

- **English**

$$A = 3.14 \times 3 \text{ in.} \times 3 \text{ in.}$$
$$3.14 \times 3 \text{ in.} = 9.42 \text{ in.}$$
$$A = 9.42 \text{ in.} \times 3 \text{ in.}$$
$$= 28.26 \text{ in.}^2$$

- **Metric**

$$A = 3.14 \times 7.5 \text{ cm} \times 7.5 \text{ cm}$$
$$3.14 \times 7.5 \text{ cm} = 23.55 \text{ cm}$$
$$A = 23.55 \text{ cm} \times 7.5 \text{ cm}$$
$$= 176.63 \text{ cm}^2$$

The area of the circle is 28.26 in.² (176.63 cm²).

19
Dotted

Using Graph Paper to Calculate the Area of Plane Figures

What You Need to Know

The area of plane figures drawn on graph paper can be determined by knowing the area of each square on the paper. If the area of figure A in the diagram is one square unit, then the area of figure B is two square units.

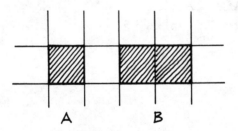

The area can also be calculated by placing dots at each vertex and using "Pick's formula," which is written:

$A = \frac{1}{2} \times b + i - 1.$

This is read: area equals one-half times b (the number of dots on the perimeter of the figure) plus i (the number of dots inside the figure) minus one.

Let's Think It Through

Calculate the area of figures C and D using Pick's formula.

1.

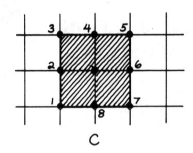

C

2.

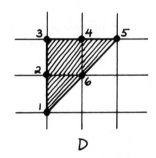

D

Answers

1. *Think!*

- Formula: $A = \frac{1}{2} \times b + i - 1$
  $$b = 8$$
  $$i = 1$$
  $$A = \frac{1}{2} \times 8 + 1 - 1$$

- The steps in solving this problem are:

  1. Multiply the first two numbers. $\frac{1}{2} \times 8 = 4$

  2. Add 1 to the product. $4 + 1 = 5$

3. Subtract 1 from the sum. 5−1 = 4

The area of figure C is 4 square units.

2. *Think!*

• Formula: A = $\frac{1}{2}$ × b + i−1
$$b = 6$$
$$i = 0$$
$$A = \frac{1}{2} \times 6 + 0−1$$

• The steps in solving this problem are:

1. Multiply the first two numbers. $\frac{1}{2}$ × 6 = 3

2. Add 0 to the product. 3 + 0 = 3

3. Subtract 1 from the sum. 3−1 = 2

The area of figure D is 2 square units.

Exercises

Use Pick's formula, A = $\frac{1}{2}$ × b + i−1, to find the area of these figures.

1.

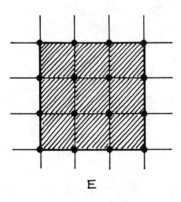

E

2.

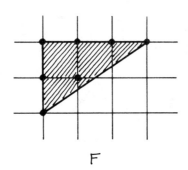

F

3.

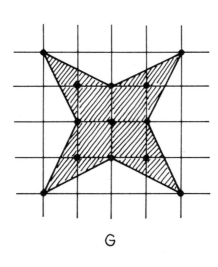

G

Activity: GEOBOARD

Purpose To build and use a geoboard to determine areas of plane geometric figures.

Materials hammer
25 3d finishing nails
block of wood at least 5 × 5 inches (12.5 × 12.5 cm) square
short rubber bands
adult helper

Procedure

1. Ask your adult helper to hammer the nails halfway into the wooden block. The nails should be driven straight, and about half their length should stick out of the wood. Position the nails so that they are 1 inch (2.5 cm) apart in the pattern shown in the diagram.

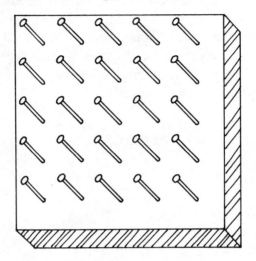

2. Stretch rubber bands around the nails to create geometric figures.

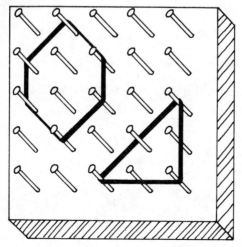

3. Use the formula A = $^1/_2$ × b + i −1 to determine the area of each figure.

Results   You have made a geoboard.

Why?   The geoboard provides a quick, fun way of designing and comparing the areas of different geometric figures. Geometric shapes are often used in art. For an extension of this activity, ask your adult helper to construct a larger, colored geoboard. Use colored rubber bands to create geometric designs and display your board. You can change the artistic design as often as you choose.

Solutions to Exercises

1. Think!

- Formula: A = $^1/_2$ × b + i−1
  b = 12
  i = 4
  A = $^1/_2$ × 12 + 4−1

- The steps in solving this problem are:

  1. Multiply the first two numbers. $^1/_2$ × 12 = 6

  2. Add 4 to the product. 6 + 4 = 10

  3. Subtract 1 from the sum. 10−1 = 9

  The area of figure E is 9 square units.

2. Think!

- Formula: A = $^1/_2$ × b + i−1
  b = 6
  i = 1
  A = $^1/_2$ × 6 + 1−1

- The steps in solving this problem are:

    1. Multiply the first two numbers. $\frac{1}{2} \times 6 = 3$

    2. Add 1 to the product. $3 + 1 = 4$

    3. Subtract 1 from the sum. $4-1 = 3$

The area of figure F is 3 square units.

3. *Think!*

- Formula: $A = \frac{1}{2} \times b + i-1$
  $$b = 8$$
  $$i = 5$$
  $$A = \frac{1}{2} \times 8 + 5-1$$
- The steps in solving this problem are:

    1. Multiply the first two numbers. $\frac{1}{2} \times 8 = 4$

    2. Add 5 to the product. $4 + 5 = 9$

    3. Subtract 1 from the sum. $9-1 = 8$

The area of figure G is 8 square units.

20
Spacey
Identifying Space Figures

What You Need to Know

When a geometric figure has three measurements—length, width, and height—it is said to be **three-dimensional** (3-D for short). Three-dimensional figures, like a box of cookies or a basketball, have tops, bottoms, fronts, backs, and sides. Mathematicians call a two-dimensional figure a plane figure, and a three-dimensional figure a **solid** or **space figure**. The five common space figures are the cone, the cylinder, the sphere, the prism, and the pyramid.

The cone, cylinder, and sphere have curved sides. A **cone** has one circular base and is shaped like an ice cream cone without the scoop of ice cream. A **cylinder** has two congruent circular bases (top and bottom) and is shaped like a can. A **sphere** has no flat bases and all points on its surface are an equal distance from its center. A sphere is shaped like a ball.

CONE

CYLINDER

SPHERE

Prisms and pyramids are made up of polygons. In a **prism** the sides are parallelograms and the two parallel bases are congruent. The most common prism is the **cube**, a space figure with six congruent square **faces** (a flat surface or plane region of a space figure). The shape of the bases is used to name other prisms, such as the *triangular prism*, *rectangular prism*, or *hexagonal prism*, among others.

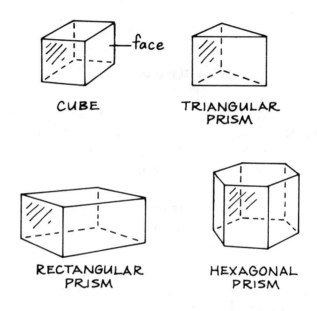

CUBE   TRIANGULAR
              PRISM

RECTANGULAR   HEXAGONAL
PRISM   PRISM

A **pyramid** has triangular sides and a single polygonal base. The shape of the base is used to name the figure, such as the *square pyramid* or *rectangular pyramid*, among others.

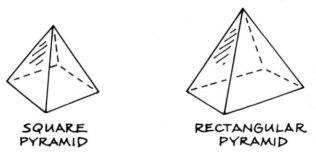

SQUARE   RECTANGULAR
PYRAMID   PYRAMID

Let's Think It Through

Identify each numbered space figure in the drawing.

Answers

1. *Think!*

- What is the shape of the hat? It has curved sides and one circular base.
- What name is given to space figures with this shape?

Figure 1 is a cone.

2. *Think!*

- What is the shape of the baseball? It is curved on all sides, with no flat bases and all points on its surface an equal distance from its center.
- What name is given to space figures with this shape?

Figure 2 is a sphere.

3. *Think!*

- What is the shape of the can of soup? It has curved sides and two congruent circular bases.
- What name is given to space figures with this shape?

Figure 3 is a cylinder.

4. *Think!*

- What is the shape of the box of cookies? The sides, top, and base are all rectangles.
- What name is given to space figures with this shape?

Figure 4 is a rectangular prism.

Exercise

Each space figure in the first column of the table can be made by folding one of the patterns shown in the third column. Match the patterns with the figures.

SPACE FIGURE	NAME	PATTERN
1.	 cube	A 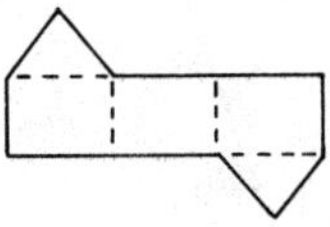
2.	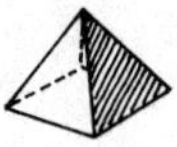 square pyramid	B 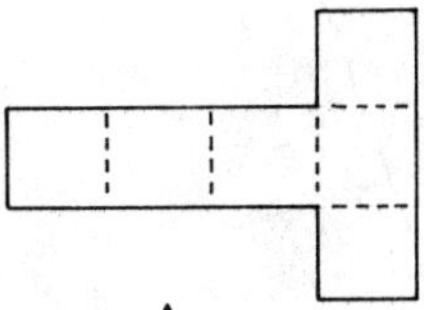
3.	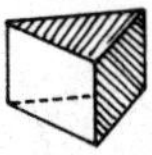 triangular prism	C 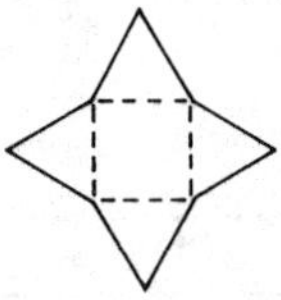

Activity: 3-D

Purpose To construct a model of a triangular prism.

Materials typing paper
  marking pen
  scissors
  ruler
  transparent tape

Procedure

1. Lay the paper over the pattern of the model.

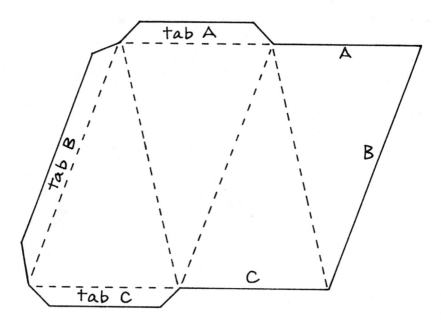

2. Trace the pattern onto the paper with the pen.

3. Cut out the traced pattern along the solid lines.

4. Make the dashed lines easier to fold by following these steps:

  • Place the edge of the ruler along one of the dashed lines.

  • With the ruler's edge as a guide, use the pen to mark back and forth across the line.

  • Repeat the procedure for each dashed line.

5. Fold along each dashed line.

6. Tape the tab sections, matching tabs to sides as follows:

- tab A over side A
- tab B over side B
- tab C over side C

Results   A model of a triangular pyramid is constructed.

Why?   The base of the pyramid as well as the sides are all triangles. The triangular sides and the single polygonal base identify the structure as a pyramid. The triangular base distinguishes the model from other pyramids.

Solutions to Exercises

1. *Think!*

- Describe the number and shape of the figure's sides and bases. Six squares.

- Which pattern has six squares?

Pattern B matches figure 1.

2. *Think!*

- Describe the number and shapes of the figure's sides and base. Four triangles and one square.

- Which pattern has these shapes in these numbers?

Pattern C matches figure 2.

3. *Think!*

- Describe the number and shapes of the figure's sides and base. Three rectangles and two triangles.

- Which pattern has these shapes in these numbers?

Pattern A matches figure 3.

21
Faces

Determining the Number of Faces, Edges, and Vertices of a Polyhedron

What You Need to Know

Each flat surface, or plane, of a space figure is called a face. The line segment where two faces meet is called an **edge**. The corner point where three or more edges meet is called a vertex. A **polyhedron** is a space figure with faces that are polygons.

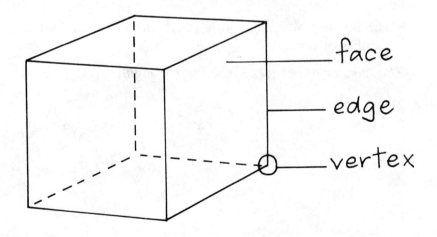

Let's Think It Through

The box shown in the diagram is a polyhedron. Examine the diagram to determine the number of its:

1. vertices

2. edges

3. faces

Answers

1. *Think!*

  • The number of vertices in a polyhedron is equal to the number of corners.

  The number of vertices for the box is eight.

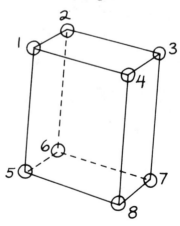

2. *Think!*

- An edge is a line segment where two faces of a polyhedron meet.

The number of edges on the box is twelve.

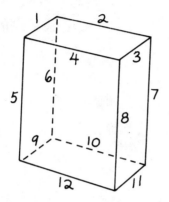

3. *Think!*

- Each flat surface of a polyhedron is a face.
- The box has a top, bottom, left side, right side, front, and back, as shown in the diagram.

The number of faces for the box is six.

	TOP		
3 LEFT SIDE	5 FRONT	4 RIGHT SIDE	6 BACK
	2 BOTTOM		

Exercise

Study the closed and open diagrams of each polyhedron and give the numbers needed to complete the table.

	Total Number of:		
Polyhedron	**Vertices**	**Edges**	**Faces**
1. Square pyramid	?	?	?
2. Triangular prism	?	?	?

Activity: FACE PRINTS

Purpose To make prints of the faces of different shaped polyhedrons.

Materials marking pen
         ruler
         rectangular dishwashing sponge
         scissors
         3 different colors of poster paint
         3 small bowls
         2 sheets of white construction paper

Procedure

1. Use the pen and ruler to draw a rectangle and a triangle on one of the largest faces of the sponge.

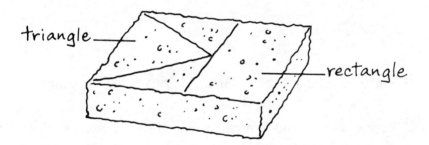

2. Cut out the two shapes drawn on the sponge. The triangle will form a triangular prism, and the rectangle will form a rectangular prism.

3. Pour about ¹/₂ inch (1.25 cm) of paint into each bowl, one color in each bowl. Use a different color of paint for each different shape or size of face.

4. Look at the faces. Dip one of the large rectangular faces of the rectangular prism into one of the bowls of paint, and make a print of this face on the paper.

5. Turn the sponge over and make a print of the opposite face using the same color of paint.

6. Repeat steps 4 and 5 to make prints of the remaining faces of the rectangular prism. Use a different color of paint for each shape of face.

7. Repeat steps 4 and 5 to make prints of each face of the triangular prism. Again, use a different color of paint for each shape of face.

Results   Six prints with one kind of shape are made by the rectangular prism. Five prints with two different kinds of shapes are made by the triangular prism.

Why?   The cuts made in the sponge may not produce faces and edges that are exactly smooth and straight, but two general shapes—rectangle and triangle—are produced. Six rectangles make up the faces of the rectangular prism, and the faces of the triangular prism are made up of two triangles and three rectangles.

Solution to Exercise

Polyhedron	Total Number of:		
	Vertices	**Edges**	**Faces**
1. Square pyramid	5	8	5
2. Triangular prism	6	9	5

22

On the Surface

Calculating the Surface Area of Rectangular Boxes

What You Need to Know

The **surface area** of a solid is the sum of the areas of all its faces. The surface area of a rectangular box is equal to the sum of the areas of the six faces that make up the box. Graph paper can be used to draw the flattened shape of the box and calculate the total surface area of the box. For the activities in this chapter, allow the length of one square on the graph paper to equal 1 inch (2.5 cm) on the box.

Let's Think It Through

Use graph paper to determine the surface area of the gift box.

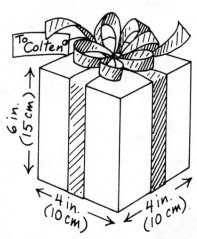

Answer

Think!

- Draw the flattened box on graph paper as in the diagram.

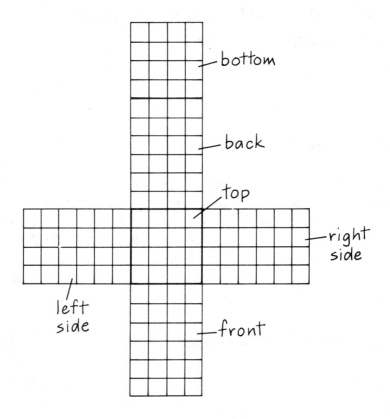

- The length of each square on the graph paper represents a length of 1 inch (2.5 cm) on the box.
- The area of each square on the graph paper represents an area on the box of:

  - **English**

  1 in. × 1 in. = 1 in.^{2}

- **Metric**

2.5 cm × 2.5 cm = 6.25 cm^2

- To calculate the surface area of the box, determine the total number of squares in the diagram and multiply the number by the area represented by one square.

Bottom area	=	16 squares
Back area	=	24 squares
Top area	=	16 squares
Front area	=	24 squares
Left-side area	=	24 squares
Right-side area	=	24 squares
Total	=	128 squares

- The surface area of the box equals the total number of squares multiplied by the area represented by one square:

  - **English**

  Surface area = 128 squares × 1 in.^{2}
  = 128 in.^{2}

- **Metric**

  Surface area = 128 squares × 6.25 cm^2
  = 800 cm^2

The surface area of the gift box is 128 in.^{2} (800 cm^2).

Exercise

Use graph paper to determine the surface area of the open shoe box.

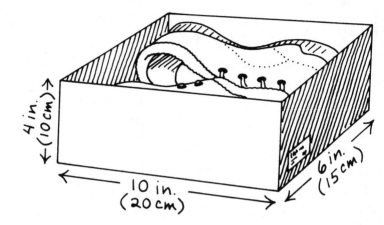

Activity: MORE SPACE

Purpose To demonstrate how surface area can be decreased.

Materials typing paper
pencil
ruler
scissors
transparent tape

Procedure

1. Lay the paper over the pattern of the cube.

2. Use the pencil and the ruler as a guide to trace the pattern on the paper four times.

3. Cut each tracing out of the paper along the solid lines.

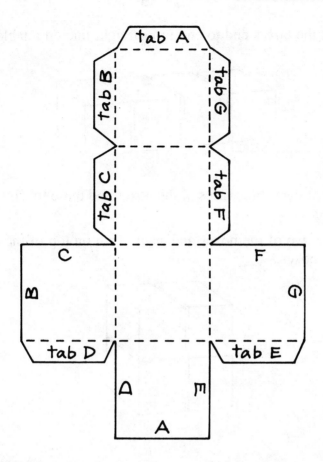

4. With the dashed lines facing you, fold each pattern along the dashed lines. Make all folds without turning the paper over.

5. Tape the tab sections to form four closed boxes, matching tabs to sides as follows:

   • tab A over side A

   • tab B over side B

   • tab C over side C

   • tab D over side D

   • tab E over side E

6. Lay the boxes end to end in a straight line on a table.

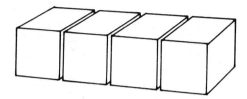

7. Count the visible faces of the boxes and those touching the table.

8. Take two of the boxes and stack them on top of the other two boxes.

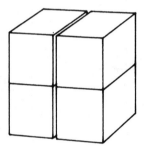

9. Again count the visible faces of the boxes and those touching the table.

Results   The boxes positioned in a straight line have 18 visible faces. The stacked boxes have 16 visible faces.

Why?   Neither the shape nor the size of the four individual boxes changes. Rearranging the boxes does not change the total size of the figure created, but the shape and therefore the surface area does change. Both figures created by combining the boxes are rectangular prisms, but the figure made up of one layer of boxes has the greatest exposed surface area.

Solution to Exercise

Think!

- Each square on the graph paper represents an area of 1 in.^{2} (6.25 cm^2) on the open shoe box.

- The total number of squares in the diagram of the box drawn on the graph paper is:

Back area	=	40 squares
Bottom area	=	60 squares
Front area	=	40 squares
Left-side area	=	24 squares
Right-side area	=	24 squares
Total	=	188 squares

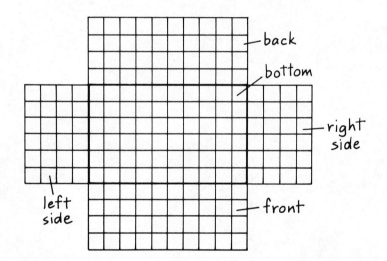

- The surface area of the box equals the total number of squares multiplied by the area represented by one square:

Surface area = 188 squares $\times$ 1 in.^{2} (6.25 cm^2)

= 188 in.^{2} (1,175 cm^2)

The surface area of the open shoe box is 188 in.^{2} (1,175 cm^2).

23
Toothpick Magic
Changing Geometric Figures Through Analysis and Reasoning

What You Need to Know

This chapter shows you how to change one geometric figure to another by moving a specified number of lines. Your mental processes of analysis and reasoning will be used and developed. To **analyze** is to mentally separate a thing into the parts of which it is composed. To **reason** is to use one's mental powers to draw conclusions. The strategy used to solve each problem in this chapter will be first to analyze the problem, and then to reason through the steps that need to be taken to make the specified change.

Let's Think It Through

Arrange 12 toothpicks as shown in the diagram. Then, rearrange any four of the toothpicks to change the four congruent squares into three congruent squares.

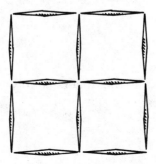

Answer

Think!

- It takes four toothpicks to make a square. Thus, the four removed toothpicks can be arranged to make one square.

- To make the three specified squares, two original squares must remain unchanged.

- Which four toothpicks when removed from the original arrangement will leave two squares?

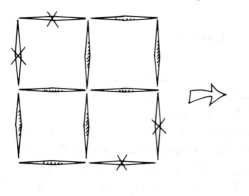

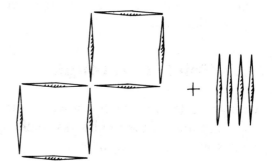

- The third square can be made at any corner of the two unchanged squares.

Two possible arrangements are:

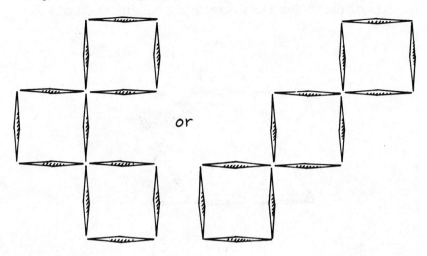

or

Exercises

For each exercise use the specified number of toothpicks to make the original figure. Then, remove or rearrange the toothpicks as directed to create the new figure.

1. Change the nine congruent squares into five congruent squares by removing four toothpicks.

2. Eighteen toothpicks make the six-pointed star. Rearrange six of the toothpicks to create six congruent diamonds.

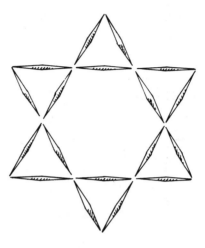

Activity: STAR BURST

Purpose To watch five toothpicks move by themselves into a six-pointed star pattern.

Materials 5 round wooden toothpicks
12-inch (30-cm) square wax paper
eyedropper
cup of water

Procedure

1. Bend each toothpick into a V shape without breaking it apart.

2. Place the bent toothpicks on the sheet of wax paper in a star burst pattern as shown in the diagram. Put the bent parts as close together as possible in the center.

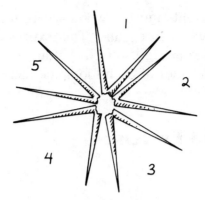

3. Fill the eyedropper with water from the cup.

4. Place four drops of water in the opening in the center of the star burst. You want the water to touch the bent part of each toothpick.

5. Watch and wait until all movement stops.

Results Each bent toothpick moves so that the angle between the two sides of the V increases. The first pattern that takes shape is a five-pointed figure similar in appearance to a starfish. The angles continue to enlarge until all motion ceases, and a fully developed five-pointed star is created.

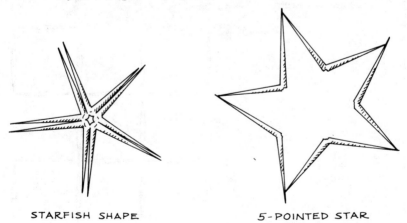

STARFISH SHAPE   5-POINTED STAR

Why? Water entering the wood where the toothpick is bent causes the wood to expand. This expansion makes the toothpick start to return to its original straight state. Thus, the angle between the sides of each toothpick increases, creating an ever-widening star.

Solutions to Exercises

1. *Think!*

- Remove the middle toothpick from each outside edge of the figure. Five congruent squares are left.

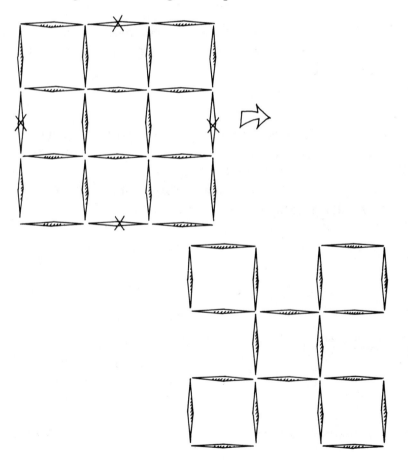

2. *Think!*

- Rotate the six toothpicks that are inside the star so that
  their ends touch in the center of the figure. Six congruent quadrilaterals are created.

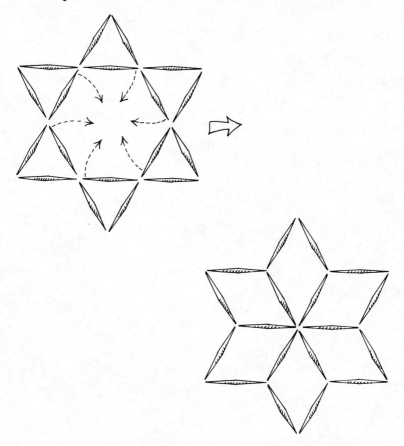

24
Over and Up

Using Coordinates to Graph Figures

What You Need to Know

Figures can be created on a grid by connecting coordinate points in order. **Coordinates** are number pairs that tell the location of a point on a grid. To graph a coordinate, follow these steps:

A. Start at the zero corner of the grid.

B. Move to the right the number of spaces equal to the first coordinate number.

C. Move up the number of spaces equal to the second coordinate number, and mark a dot on the grid.

The diagram shows the steps for graphing coordinates (2, 5).

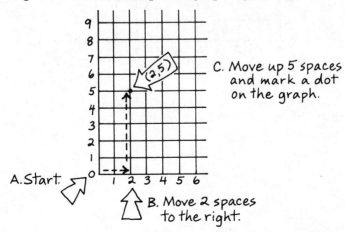

Let's Think It Through

1. Graph these coordinates and connect their points in the order given to create a figure: (3, 5), (4, 2), (8, 2), (9, 5), (6, 4).

2. Graph a similar figure, but make it twice as large.

Answers

1. *Think!*

- Follow the steps for graphing coordinates.

- Draw a line to connect each point in the order given. Close the figure by drawing a line from the last to the first point. The arrows in the diagram indicate the order in which each line is drawn.

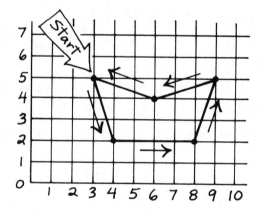

2. *Think!*

• The coordinates of a figure twice as large as the previous figure are determined by multiplying each of the coordinates of the previous figure by 2.

$(3, 5) \times 2 = (3 \times 2, 5 \times 2) = (6, 10)$
$(4, 2) \times 2 = (4 \times 2, 2 \times 2) = (8, 4)$
$(8, 2) \times 2 = (8 \times 2, 2 \times 2) = (16, 4)$
$(9, 5) \times 2 = (9 \times 2, 5 \times 2) = (18, 10)$
$(6, 4) \times 2 = (6 \times 2, 4 \times 2) = (12, 8)$

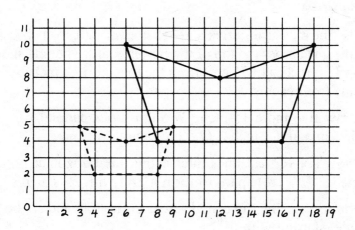

Exercises

1. Graph a figure using these coordinates: $(1, 4)$, $(2, 4)$, $(2, 1)$, $(4, 1)$, $(4, 4)$, $(5, 4)$, $(3, 6)$.

2. Graph a similar figure, but make it three times as large.

Activity: BIGGER

Purpose   To use a grid to make an enlargement of a figure.

Materials   yardstick (meterstick)
pencil
18-inch (45-cm) square poster board
marking pen
pencil with eraser
crayons

Procedure

1. Use the measuring stick and pencil to draw a 15-inch (37.5-cm) line across the top of the poster board. The line should be 1 ½ inches (3.75 cm) from the top and 1 ½ inches (3.75 cm) from each side of the paper.

2. Draw five more 15-inch (37.5 cm) lines parallel with the first line and 3 inches (7.5 cm) apart.

3. Draw six vertical lines intersecting the horizontal lines, 3 inches (7.5 cm) apart, to form a grid with 25 squares.

4. Number the lines in pencil across the bottom and up the left side, starting with 0.

5. Graph the coordinates of the figure of the boat shown on the next page onto your large grid.

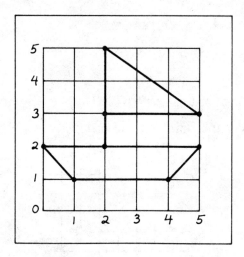

6. Trace over the pencil lines of the drawing with the pen.

7. Erase the grid lines and numbers.

8. Use the crayons to color the figure and add water waves and birds to complete the picture.

Results   An enlarged, colored picture of a boat on the water is produced.

Why?   The original figure is on a grid made of 25 congruent squares. The figure you made also has 25 squares, but they are bigger than those in the smaller grid. Using the grid with larger squares allows you to use the same coordinates to draw an enlarged version of the original boat.

Solutions to Exercises

1. *Think!*

- Use the coordinates provided to place points on the grid.
- Connect the points in the order given.

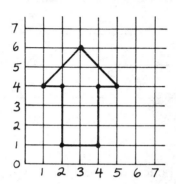

2. *Think!*

- The coordinates of a figure three times as large as the previous one are determined by multiplying each of the coordinates of the previous figure by 3.

$$(1, 4) \times 3 = (1 \times 3, 4 \times 3) = (3, 12)$$
$$(2, 4) \times 3 = (2 \times 3, 4 \times 3) = (6, 12)$$
$$(2, 1) \times 3 = (2 \times 3, 1 \times 3) = (6, 3)$$
$$(4, 1) \times 3 = (4 \times 3, 1 \times 3) = (12, 3)$$
$$(4, 4) \times 3 = (4 \times 3, 4 \times 3) = (12, 12)$$
$$(5, 4) \times 3 = (5 \times 3, 4 \times 3) = (15, 12)$$
$$(3, 6) \times 3 = (3 \times 3, 6 \times 3) = (9, 18)$$

- See diagram to compare the figures.

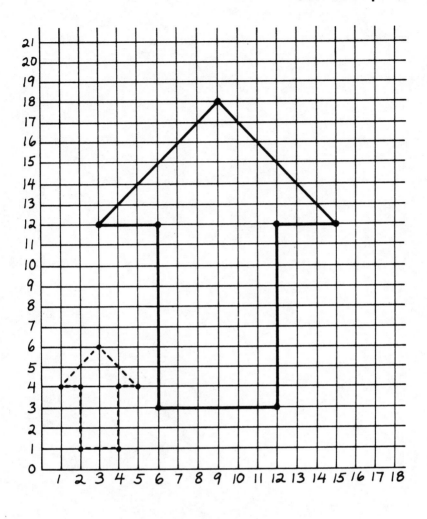

25
Three-Dimensional Drawings

Using Perspective to Draw Three-Dimensional Figures in Two Dimensions

What You Need to Know

Two-dimensional drawings of three-dimensional (3-D) objects can be made by using perspective. **Perspective** is the technique of drawing on a flat surface in such a way as to make the drawing look three-dimensional. The drawing of the pencil box is an example of the use of perspective to give a drawing the look of a 3-D figure. The lines are angled to make the box appear to have depth.

Let's Think It Through

Use a pencil, ruler, and graph paper to draw the following:

1. A rectangular prism

2. A cylinder

Answers

1. Draw the rectangular prism by following these steps:

- Draw a rectangle on graph paper with a width of five squares and a length of three squares. (NOTE: *The measurements are not significant.*)

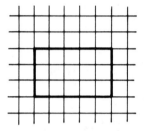

- Draw a second overlapping rectangle of equal size, but start two squares to the right and one square up from the first rectangle, as shown in the diagram.

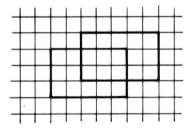

- Draw lines to connect the corresponding vertices of the two rectangles.

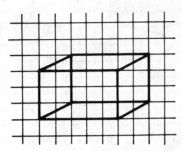

2. Draw the cylinder by following these steps:

- Draw an oval nine squares wide and two squares long. (NOTE: *The measurements are not significant.*)

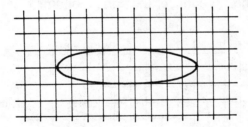

- Draw an identical oval eight squares below the first oval.

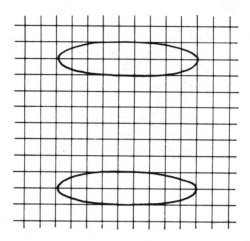

- Draw lines to connect the corresponding ends of the two ovals.

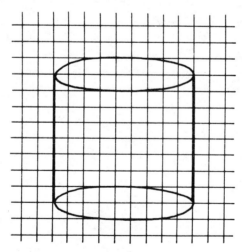

Exercises

1. Draw an open toy box.

2. Draw a cookie jar.

Activity: SWIMMING FISH

Purpose   To show how colors can be used to create a three-dimensional drawing that seems to rise off the page.

Materials   typing paper
1 pale blue and 1 pale pink highlight marker
1 red and 1 blue transparent plastic report folder

Procedure

1. Lay the paper over the diagram of the fish in the bowl.

2. Trace the fishbowl with the blue marker.

3. Trace the fish with the pink marker.

4. Place the tracing on a table.

5. Cut one 2-by-2-inch (5-by-5-cm) square from each of the folders.

6. Close your left eye and use your right eye to look through the red plastic at the tracing.

7. Close your right eye and use your left eye to look through the blue plastic at the tracing.

8. With the red plastic over your right eye and the blue plastic over your left eye, look at the tracing with both eyes.

Results   The fishbowl is darker and the pink fish disappears or is only faintly visible when viewed only through the red plastic. Through the blue plastic, the fish is darker and the blue lines of the bowl disappear or are only faintly visible. Looking through the red and blue plastic at the same time produces a 3-D image of a pink fish in a blue bowl.

Why?   What you see is an optical illusion—a misleading image seen when your brain is tricked by your eyes. The illusion in this experiment is caused by the fact that you have two eyes, each of which is sending a different image to the brain. The right eye sees a dark fishbowl and the left eye sees a dark fish. When the brain puts these two images together, a 3-D image results.

Solutions to Exercises

1. *Think!*

- What shape is an open toy box? A rectangular prism.

- Draw a rectangular prism with a width of five squares and a length of six squares, following the instructions given earlier. (NOTE: *The rectangle can be any size.*)

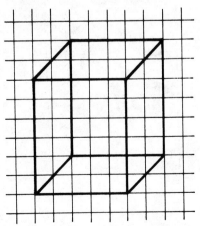

- Erase the lines indicated in the diagram.

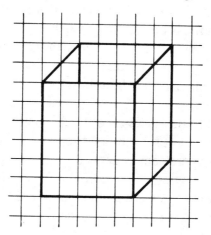

- Trace the drawing onto a sheet of typing paper. Add the label "toys" and a toy plus shading to complete the drawing. Be sure to erase any lines of the box that pass through the figure of the toy.

2. *Think!*

- What shape is a cookie jar? A cylinder.

- Draw a cylinder with a width of eight squares and a length of two squares, following the instructions given earlier. (NOTE: *The cylinder can be any size.*)

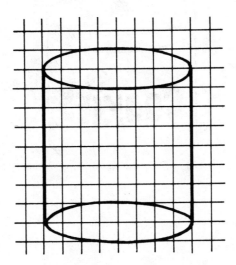

- Erase the line indicated in the diagram.

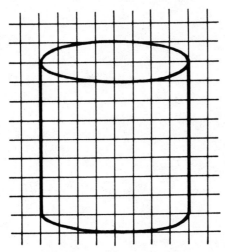

- Trace the drawing onto a sheet of typing paper. To make the lid, add a curved line and a circle as the knob. Write the word "cookies" on the jar so that the word curves as if written on a line parallel with the bottom curve and add shading.

Glossary

Acute angle: An angle that measures less than 90 degrees.

Acute triangle: A triangle in which all angles measure less than 90 degrees.

Adjacent: Adjoining; neighboring.

Affinity: The attraction of one substance to another substance.

Analyze: To mentally separate a thing into the parts of which it is composed.

Angle: The figure formed when two rays that have the same endpoint or two straight lines meet.

Area: The measure of the number of square units needed to cover the surface of a plane figure.

Central angle: An angle that has its vertex at the center of a circle.

Chord: Any line segment that begins and ends on the circumference of a circle.

Circle: A simple closed curve; a plane figure bordered by a curved line called the circumference; every point on the circumference is an equal distance from the center point of the circle.

Circumference: The perimeter of a circle; the length of this boundary.

Closed curve: A curved figure formed by a continuous line.

Closed figure: A geometric figure that begins and ends at the same point.

Complex curve: A curved figure formed by a line that intersects itself.

Cone: A space figure that has curved sides and one circular base; shaped like an ice cream cone without the scoop of ice cream.

Congruent: The same; equal to.

Congruent polygons: Polygons that are exactly the same size and shape.

Coordinates: Number pairs that tell the location of a point on a grid.

Cube: A prism with six congruent sides.

Curved figure: Any geometric figure that does not have straight sides, such as a circle; can be closed or open, simple or complex.

Cylinder: A space figure that has curved sides and two congruent circular bases; shaped like a can.

Diameter: A chord that passes through the center of a circle.

Edge: A line segment where two faces of a space figure meet.

Endpoint: A point at the end of a line segment or ray.

Equilateral triangle: A triangle with three congruent sides.

Face: A flat surface or plane region of a space figure.

Hexagon: A six-sided polygon.

Intersecting lines: Lines that meet or cross each other and have only one point in common.

Isosceles trapezoid: A trapezoid whose two nonparallel sides are congruent.

Isosceles triangle: A triangle with two congruent sides.

Line: The geometric definition of a line is a straight path that has no definite length and goes on forever in both directions; a mark made by a pen, a pencil, or other tool on a surface.

Line of symmetry: A line that divides a figure into two identical parts that are mirror images of each other; the parts match if folded along the line.

Line segment: A part of a line, which follows a straight path between two endpoints.

Möbius strip: A closed complex curve with only one side— the inside is also the outside; discovered by August Ferdinand Möbius (1790–1868).

Obtuse angle: An angle that measures greater than 90 degrees.

Obtuse triangle: A triangle with one angle that measures greater than 90 degrees.

Open curve: A curved figure formed by a noncontinuous, broken line.

Optical illusion: A misleading image seen because of misinterpretations made by the brain.

Origami: The art of folding paper into shapes that look like objects.

Parallel lines: Any two or more lines that do not intersect and are always the same distance apart.

Parallelogram: A quadrilateral that has two pairs of parallel sides; common name for a rhomboid.

Pattern: A predictable arrangement of things, such as numbers and/or geometric figures, that have some relationship to each other.

Pentagon: A five-sided polygon.

Pentomino: A figure made from five congruent squares; the entire side of one square must line up with the whole side of the square it touches.

Perimeter: The outer boundary of a plane figure; the length of this boundary.

Perpendicular lines: Two lines that intersect, forming a right angle.

Persistence of vision: The eye's ability to temporarily hold on to images after the image is out of sight.

Perspective: The technique of drawing on a flat surface in such a way as to make the drawing look three-dimensional.

Pi (π): The ratio of the circumference of any circle to its diameter; 3.14 is the common value used.

Plane figure: A geometric figure that lies on a flat surface.

Plane geometry: The study of two-dimensional figures.

Polygon: A closed plane figure formed by three or more line segments that are joined only at the endpoints, with each endpoint connected to only two line segments.

Polyhedron: A space figure with faces that are polygons.

Prism: A space figure with polygonal sides and two congruent parallel bases.

Protractor: An instrument used to measure angles in degrees.

Pyramid: A space figure that has triangular sides and a single polygonal base.

Quadrilateral: A closed plane figure formed by four line segments; a four-sided polygon; can be a trapezium, trapezoid, or parallelogram.

Radius: A line segment from a point on the circumference of a circle to the center of the circle.

Ray: A part of a line with one endpoint; it follows a straight path that goes on forever in only one direction.

Reason: To use one's mental powers to draw conclusions.

Rectangle: A parallelogram that has four right angles and only opposite sides are congruent.

Rhomboid: A parallelogram that has no right angles and only opposite sides are congruent; commonly called a parallelogram.

Rhombus: A parallelogram that has no right angles and four congruent sides.

Right angle: An angle that measures 90 degrees.

Right triangle: A triangle that has one 90-degree angle.

Scalene triangle: A triangle with no congruent sides.

Simple curve: A curved figure, such as a circle, formed by a line that does not intersect.

Solid: Another name for space figure.

Solid geometry: The study of three-dimensional figures.

Space figure: A geometric figure that is three-dimensional; also called a solid; can be a cone, cylinder, sphere, prism, or pyramid.

Sphere: A space figure that has no flat bases and all points on its curved surface are an equal distance from its center; shaped like a ball.

Square: A rectangle that has four congruent sides.

Surface area: The sum of the areas of all the faces of a solid.

Symmetric figures: Figures with lines of symmetry.

Tangram: A Chinese puzzle made by cutting a square into five triangles, a square, and a rhomboid.

Three-dimensional: Having three measurements—length, width, and height; said of space figures; 3-D for short.

Trapezium: A quadrilateral that has no parallel sides.

Trapezoid: A quadrilateral that has one pair of parallel sides.

Triangle: A polygon made up of three sides; the sum of the angles created by the three sides is always 180 degrees.

Two-dimensional: Having only two measurements—length and width; said of plane figures.

Vertex (plural **vertices**): The point where two or more rays, two or more sides of a polygon, or three or more edges of a space figure meet.

Index

Angle, 11–21, 213, 215, 217
  acute, 11, 213
  definition of. 11. 213
  example of, 11, 12
  measurement of, 12–15
  naming of, 12
  obtuse, 12, 215
  right, 12, 217
  unit, 11

Central angle:
  definition of, 83, 213
  example of, 83
  measurement of, 83–93
Circle:
  area of, 145–154
  central angle, 83–93, 213
  chord, 75, 213
  definition of, 65, 213
  diameter, 75, 214
  example of, 75
  parts of, 75–82
  radius, 75, 216
Closed figure, 29, 214
Curved figure, 65–82, 213,
    214, 215, 217
  circle, 65, 75–82
  closed, 65, 66, 67, 213
  complex, 65, 66. 67. 214
  definition of, 65, 214

examples of, 65–72
Möbius strip, 69–72, 215
open, 65, 215
simple, 65, 66, 67, 217

Graphing, 195–202

Intersecting lines, 21–27, 214
  definition of, 21, 214
  examples of, 21, 22, 23

Lines, 5–10, 215
  definition of, 5, 215
  example of, 5
  intersecting, 21–27, 214
  naming of, 5
  parallel, 21–27, 215
  perpendicular, 21–27, 216
  symmetry, 103–111, 215
Line segment, 5–10, 215
  definition of, 5, 215
  example of, 5, 6, 7
  naming of, 5

Möbius strip, 69–72, 215

Optical illusion, 8–9, 207–209,
    215
  definition of, 9, 215
  example of, 9, 207–209

More Exciting and Fun Activity Books
from Janice VanCleave . . .
Available from your local bookstore
or simply use the order form below.

Mail to: Jennifer Bergman, John Wiley and Sons, Inc.,
605 Third Avenue, New York, New York, 10158

Title	ISBN	Price
__ ANIMALS	55052-3	$9.95
__ EARTHQUAKES	57107-5	$9.95
__ ELECTRICITY	31010-7	$9.95
__ GRAVITY	55050-7	$9.95
__ MACHINES	57108-3	$9.95
__ MAGNETS	57106-7	$9.95
__ MICROSCOPES	58956-X	$9.95
__ MOLECULES	55054-X	$9.95
__ VOLCANOES	30811-0	$9.95
__ ASTRONOMY	53573-7	$10.95
__ BIOLOGY	50381-9	$10.95
__ CHEMISTRY	62085-8	$10.95
__ DINOSAURS	30812-9	$10.95
__ EARTH SCIENCE	53010-7	$10.95
__ GEOGRAPHY	59842-9	$10.95
__ GEOMETRY	31141-3	$10.95
__ MATH	54265-2	$10.95
__ PHYSICS	52505-7	$10.95
__ 200 GOOEY, SLIPPERY, SLIMY, WEIRD, & FUN EXPERIMENTS	57921-1	$12.95
__ 201 AWESOME, MAGICAL, BIZARRE, INCREDIBLE EXPERIMENTS	31011-5	$12.95

To Order
by Phone:

Call
1-800-225-5945

Total:_____

Wiley pays postage & handling for prepaid orders
[ ] Check/Money order enclosed
[ ] Charge my: [ ]VISA   [ ]MASTERCARD   [ ]AMEX   [ ]DISCOVER
Card #:_____ Expiration Date:_____/_____
NAME:_____
ADDRESS:_____
CITY/STATE/ZIP:_____
SIGNATURE:_____
(Order not valid unless signed)

WILEY
Publishers Since 1807